Learning to Interpret Toward Love

Actually Embracing People of Different Sexuality (in the kind of churches where they haven't been)

For Javen,
It's an honour for me to be asked to send you this book. With respect & best wishes,

Peter Fitch

Peter Fitch

Copyright © 2013 by Peter Fitch
ISBN-13: 978-1490402857

All rights reserved. The author retains international copyright. Written permission must be secured from the publisher to use or reproduce any part of this book, except for brief quotations in critical reviews or articles.

Produced by CreateSpace.com in the United States

Layout, cover design: Brad Jersak.
Cover Art: Mary Ellen Fitch, photo of painting by Heather Mercer, St. Croix Vineyard Café, St. Stephen, NB. UBP.

All Scripture quotations, unless otherwise indicated, are taken from the New American Standard Bible®, Copyright © 1960, 1962, 1963, 1968, 1971, 1972, 1973, 1975, 1977, 1995 by The Lockman Foundation. Used by permission. (www.lockman.org).

Other Bible Versions referenced:

Holy Bible, NEW INTERNATIONAL READER'S VERSION®. © 1996, 1998 Biblica. All rights reserved throughout the world. Used by permission of Biblica.

New King James Version®. Copyright © 1982 by Thomas Nelson, Inc. Used by permission. All rights reserved.

New Revised Standard Version Bible, copyright © 1989, the Division of Christian Education of the National Council of the Churches of Christ in the United States of America. Used by permission. All rights reserved.

Scripture taken from NET Bible® copyright ©1996-2006 by Biblical Studies Press, L.L.C. http://netbible.com All rights reserved.

The-volution Press
To contact the author:
email: pfitch7@gmail.com

DEDICATION

For Jack and Quil,
and everyone who has provoked
my thinking on these issues,
either by example or in print.
Thank you for believing
in a better way.

ABOUT THE AUTHOR

Peter Fitch (D.Min., Fuller) has been teaching at St. Stephen's University in St. Stephen, New Brunswick, Canada, since 1979. He is currently Dean of Ministry Studies, with courses in Religious Studies, Philosophy and Postmodern Christianity. He has also taught in college or university programs in the United States, New Zealand, Hong Kong, and the United Kingdom. A major focus in all his academic work has been the history of Christian spirituality. Peter and his wife, Mary Ellen, along with a group of friends, planted St. Croix Vineyard Church in 1992, and they continue to share in pastoral leadership there. They have four grown children: Hannah (married to Will, parents of Sophie and Ari), Noah (married to Cara), Zoe (married to Dave) and Isaac.

TABLE OF CONTENTS

Preface 1

Chapter One: Rules or People? 3

Chapter Two: Interpreting Toward Love 17

Chapter Three: And What Does the Bible Say? 43

Chapter Four: The Story Behind My Changing View 71

Chapter Five: Can We Really Have New Thoughts? 113

Chapter Six: What Is the Importance of the Bible? 123

Chapter Seven: Bringing It Home 131

Endnotes 137

Selected Bibliography 145

PREFACE

As is evident in what follows, I've been helped by many people to come to a changed perspective related to LGBT people and church, and I am very grateful. Some are mentioned in this book. Many are not. Brian McLaren helped me to adjust my thinking about the Bible, although I believed I had been working with a healthy view. Wendy Gritter helped me to see the need for "generous spaciousness," and then for something more. She gave words to feelings in a way that made sense. Justin Lee provided a powerful case study in his book about his own life. Many students and friends allowed me to process my thoughts out loud. Ron Alberts, especially, encouraged me to write. The students whose stories I share were a profound influence. My brother, Jack, has been a friend and mentor. My wife, Mary Ellen, has walked every part of this journey with me. She is a natural theologian, walking the better paths without the bother of many words.

I am grateful, too, for the open atmosphere in our communities at St. Stephen's University and St. Croix Vineyard. People wrestle with ideas and come to different conclusions, but all are accepted and valued in spite of contrary opinions. Mary Ellen and I share life with, and are taught by, many people. In particular, we have had the privilege of working and laughing with Walter and Carol Thiessen for decades.

Nancy Verrall Warren, professional editor, and Brad Jersak, writer and publisher, both gave invaluable help to the style of this book. More than that, as friends who encouraged ongoing dialogue, they each contributed to the content as well. Of course, the conclusions within these pages are mine. Others will have to tell their own stories. Some of my closest friends and colleagues in both my church and academic life share my concerns but not my sense of what to do about them. It is a privilege to struggle forward into life with people of such quality, even when we disagree.

Peter Fitch
St. Stephen, New Brunswick

Chapter One
Rules or People?

It has taken me a long time. I've struggled and wrestled with an appropriate way to reflect Christ's love to people with different sexuality. I have always wanted our church to be open and welcoming to all, but I've struggled with imaginary dialogues. Many pastors will relate:

> LGBT people are welcome here, but what happens if they want to lead in some way? What if they want to be on a worship band, or lead a small group? Will they want to stay if they discover that there's a glass ceiling? But how can there not be? Their orientation is a symptom of brokenness—how can we let them model leadership to everyone else if their life is built upon sin?

I think my biggest stumbling block to inclusivity has been a desire to remain faithful to Scripture. I love the Bible. I spent years in seminaries learning how to translate it and interpret it, and I've taught at a Christian university for almost three and a half decades. I've been a pastor for more than two and a half decades. I love philosophy, theology and history, but most of my work in church or at school is related quite directly to Bible teaching. What a struggle it has been to reach beyond the clear-seeming inferences of Scripture!

I've never felt entirely comfortable with a good deal of the political baggage in conservative Christian circles, but I definitely think like a conservative Christian in some of my most basic theological assumptions. I "gave my life" to Jesus as a teenager during the first year of my university experience. I had an amazing conversion encounter that convinced me that I had found and been transformed by a living God. I have been walking into the relationship that was at least partly initiated at that time for more than 40 years. I can never stop being grateful for what this relationship has meant to me. It's richer now than ever, and although I understand this will be difficult for people without belief of their own to accept, the sense of partnership with God in work and play is almost overwhelming as it grows.

I say all of this so that it will be clear to anyone reading that I have a belief system that is formed around Scripture. I also have a community of friends around the world that will have a very hard time with conclusions I will present in this book. Some will have travelled a similar journey and will smile. Others will shake their heads. Some may feel betrayed. But I have to share what I've been thinking about. I sincerely believe that it is the path of faithfulness to God.

Christian thinking has been responsible for many wonderful acts of sacrifice and love in the world; it has also led, even when intentions were honourable, to some terrible outcomes. Here's a short list: crusades, anti-Semitism (including countless acts of violence), inquisitions, racism (including segregated societies), oppression of women, colonialism, and residential schools. I could go on. My temptation, as a young person, was to believe that any horrible results had been carried out by those who merely professed Christian faith. In other words, bad things done in the name of Christ were done by people within the church who were not true Christians. Now, after years of reading the works of famous believers from all periods of church history, I understand something of the naivety of this position.

I have come to the conclusion that the attempt to exclude sincere Christians of different sexual orientation or practice from full standing in faith communities is a serious mistake. It has led to many tragic acts. Some of these are subtle: children from conservative religious backgrounds who self-identify as LGBT people are many times more likely to attempt suicide than people from more neutral backgrounds.[1] That in itself ought to cause us to reconsider staunchly held positions: the fruit is not all good.

But what about the Bible? How can a community of people who long to be faithful to Scripture welcome and share life with people whose orientations go dramatically against the standards given in their sacred texts? What follows is an explanation of why I think this is necessary and how I ended up in such a position.

Early Perspectives

I don't think I ever felt too strongly against homosexuality as I was growing up. I shared the perspective of my culture at the time that it was different than normal, but I don't think I was exposed to very much. This changed when I went to university. Gay groups and parties were publicly presented. I had friends who gradually began to identify as gay or bisexual. I didn't think too much about it. For me, life was filled with Bible studies and Christian groups and everything seemed new and exciting; my focus was largely there.

After a couple of years in a public university in Canada I began to do Christian study in the United States. I finished my first degree at a college in Minnesota and then began graduate studies at a seminary in Colorado. I guess it was inevitable that I would begin to accept the "normal" Christian way of looking at this issue.

It was probably 10 years later that my older brother told us that he was gay and that he had found a partner. I think this was really hard for my parents to accept, but I remember hearing that my father told my mother, "I refuse to lose a son." Dad came from a family that had some long-standing feuds. I've always been grateful that he avoided that tendency. From that moment on, he accepted and honoured both my brother and his partner, who have been together now for about three decades.

After my dad died, my brother asked my other brother and me how we felt about his life. We answered that we loved them both. Uncomfortably, he asked each of us directly, challenging us to know our personal thoughts about their orientation. When it was my turn, I said something like this:

> I love you. I love you both. There is absolutely nothing in me that doesn't want to support you guys. On the other hand, I have been formed by the Scriptures and they are life to me. I am so torn; I feel crucified between these things.

All I remember after that is my brother embracing me. He said, "You're a good man, Pete." This meant the world to me. I had feared that my honest expression of struggle would alienate us. Instead, he honoured my pain and met me where I was. He reached across the divide.

Through the Years

Occasionally a student or a church person would come out to me. I always tried to listen with understanding. I tried to communicate acceptance of each person without saying that I fully accepted his or her orientation. Sometimes I offered to pray for people, hoping, I guess, that God would miraculously enter the situation and "heal" them. In one case, this seemed to happen. A woman who had left her husband after a traumatic loss of a child had entered several lesbian relationships. After hours of listening and praying together over a period of about a year, she told my wife and me that all she wanted was to go home. We encouraged her to ask her husband if he would take her back. He did, and they managed to rebuild their life together. I believe they are both still happy about this, many years later.

But there were others. No matter how much listening took place, or how many prayers were said, no change took place in their orientation or outlook. I was mystified. Why didn't it work? If this was sin, why didn't it go away after it was confessed? If this was emotional brokenness, why wasn't it healed? I don't mean to be simplistic here. Real problems of any sort are not easily dealt with. However, the lack of demonstrable change in issues regarding orientation acted as a pearl in the oyster shell for me. It was an irritant in one way, but I think it was helpful in producing a better, perhaps beautiful, understanding over time.

Gradually I came to realize that there was nothing in me that wanted to change anyone while we were actually together. It was different when I thought about this away from real people—then I could hold on to a belief system in an abstract way. But my heart felt consistently drawn toward acceptance of people while I was in their presence. As far as I could tell, it seemed that God felt the same way. When I think of this now, I'm reminded of Pascal's saying: "the heart has its reasons, which reason does not know."[2] He was speaking about believing in God in spite of intellectual struggles, but I can see an analogy here. My intuition was able to accept people before my reason could reconcile this with the Scriptures. At times the heart is a better theologian than the brain.

Incarnational Theology

I taught theological subjects for almost a decade before I became a pastor. I remember being surprised when I began to lead a church that there was such a difference between the pursuits. Probably it should have been obvious: real people, real problems. I know that some people feel that there ought not to be such a distinction. Theology sets the standard and people ought to be encouraged to meet it. Something in me believed right from the start that this was exactly the wrong way to pastor people. Instead, it seemed to me, my job was to encourage people to receive the love of God exactly as they were. No matter what they were working through, no matter how many addictions or issues, it was always the same: help them to understand that God loves them *now*. There is nothing that needs to happen before they begin to feel His love. Once God's love is received, some very wonderful transformations can begin. A soul, feeling rooted and grounded in the security that this experience brings, can begin to reflect honestly on areas where growth is needed. And then, it starts. Connected to the Source, it seems as though there is strength to change, power to become better than before. It's not magic, but it is real.

To me, this is similar to the direction that Jesus modelled in becoming human. The word "incarnate" means "in flesh." Christianity is a celebration of God coming to where we are. It is all about meeting people with acceptance and grace before they are whole or healthy or mature. True pastoral care, as Thomas Oden says, is always like the movement in the Apostles' Creed: Jesus dies, is buried and on the third day He is raised from the dead. In a similar way we enter into the pain and death that people experience before we join with them in a resurrection of new hope.[3] The thing that makes it possible is empathy. Oden calls this the precondition of all therapeutic effectiveness, and he defines it as the ability to enter imaginatively into the perceptual framework of the other.[4] This is what God does with us. He enters our life, with all of its issues, and He communicates grace and acceptance, not rules and judgment. We have to do this, too.

Centred Set Groups

This decision to bring God's love and acceptance to people at their place of need, rather than encouraging them to change in order to be worthy, fits well with a concept that has been popular in church-planting circles for the past few decades. It is the belief that most groups, whether religious or political or cultural, tend to default into bounded sets, but that a centred set[5] approach would be better.

Bounded sets have a clear line around them, with a strong sense of "we" and "they," or "us" and "them." It's very easy to see who fits within a bounded set. Some indicators could be language, style, customs, behaviour, or belief. People who are comfortable within a bounded set often exude confidence and familiarity with all that is going on. But there are some problems. First, these groups can have an unattractive air of exclusivity, making newcomers feel that it's hard to fit in. Second, all evaluations of whether or not someone fits are external; there is no way to know where someone's heart is pointed. He or she may look perfect according to the chosen standards but be contemplating or practicing actions that would shock everyone else. Third, it's very difficult to be honest and vulnerable with others if you are having doubts or issues with the group's belief or values. A certain degree of performance is necessary in order to fully belong to a group like this; any failure in the group's eyes can lead to a diminished position. For this reason, it's almost impossible for a leader to be vulnerable.

An opposite extreme to a bounded set might be called a fuzzy set. The characteristic of this kind of group is obscurity of direction. Fuzzy sets can be chaotic; it's hard to tell if they stand for anything distinct from the rest of culture or from the general environment. There is an absence of clarity about what the group is trying to accomplish, or how it means to go about its task. Everyone fits, but where is it headed?

Centred sets are different. They exist in the middle of these extremes. All that is important in a centred set is the centre that people are aiming for. In a religious group, the centre might be defined as "becoming like Christ." There is a boundary around the group's values, for it is trying to help people grow in a certain direction. But the boundary is a dotted line, not the impenetrable barrier of the bounded set. People belong to the group from the first moment that they would like to, no matter if their behaviours or beliefs are not in line with what the group is trying to accomplish. As they begin to point toward the centre, they are accepted as valued members right away. They belong. This means that they are welcome along with their addictions and problems. The hope and belief of the group is that a certain level of wholeness and healing will come as people follow their heart toward the identified centre. It's possible for anyone, even a leader, to be very honest in this kind of system about what's really going on in life. Belonging is immediate; it will not easily be lost. People are free to share their real-life struggles and issues. This, in turn, has the effect of making others feel welcome in their own imperfect condition.

Belonging Before Believing

Another way to express all of this has emerged out of discussions regarding the difference in perspective between European western heritage Christian faith and Celtic Christianity. Before the influence of Roman Christianity became widespread in what is now the UK and Ireland, there was an earlier form that was developed and maintained by Irish monks. A danger exists in romanticizing this form, but it seems to contain some different and positive attitudes toward art, nature, women (who sometimes led the communities) and the holiness of all things. A very great difference seems apparent when one studies the nature of Roman Benedictine monasticism, which often withdrew from the world, and Celtic monasteries, which were placed at the intersection of church and culture in order to care for people and educate them. Instead of imposing new and alien forms of worship on people, Celtic monks seemed better at adapting worship of Christ to existing ways. The Druids had worshipped outside; so did the Celtic monks. Because they reached toward culture without a wholesale rejection of what was there, they were very successful in winning the hearts and minds of the populace. It is tempting to speculate that Celtic Christians might have done a better job of bringing Christ to the indigenous cultures around the world than the Roman western heritage faith that actually made it to these places.

How does this provide another way to speak of the value of centred sets? Many forms of Christianity have preached a message at people with the hope that it would be believed, that it would affect behaviour, and that it would lead to belonging in the church. It seems as though Celtic groups lived the reverse of this notion: people belonged right away, with the hope that participation in life together would affect everyone's behaviour, and that this, in turn, would lead to belief in a real God who expressed Himself through the care of the community.[6] It wasn't "believe, behave, belong"; rather, it was "belong, behave, believe."

But Not With This Issue!

Strangely, I have known many Christians who would acknowledge all that I have just written until it comes to full inclusion in the church of LGBT people. A great fear exists that embracing homosexuals into the church will lead to a disregard of the Bible. I think that's why it's so difficult for so many. And I understand this. I didn't come to my own relationship with God through the Bible, but it was the Bible that helped me to understand and develop the relationship. If the Bible is seen as wrong at this point, how will it maintain relevance for future generations?

Chapter Two
Interpreting Toward Love

Not a Rulebook

I believe that there are several levels of misunderstanding that are prevalent in all discussions of interpretation from an extremely conservative point of view. In other words, it is my suspicion that the very best of intentions have at times borne poor results. Loving the Bible so much has led a great many people to miss its intent and focus while doing their best to capture "chapter and verse" on every subject.

Jesus might have said it this way (as He did), "straining out a gnat, they swallow a camel ..." (Matt. 23:24). Members of the Jewish sect that He most often criticized, the Pharisees, were famous for studying and disputing about their Scriptures, our Old Testament. They were determined to get it right. Many were legalistic in interpretation, and judgmental of those who disagreed with them. In their attempts to make sure that nothing damaged their digestive purity ("straining out a gnat") they missed the things that Jesus had just described as "the weightier provisions of the law." He called these justice, mercy and faithfulness (Matt. 23:23).

In other words, the Bible is the kind of book that can be mishandled if you hold it too tightly. By trying to obey each individual comment, you can miss the heart of the message. In fact, I think that a great deal of troubled interpretation is impossible to avoid if you think of the Bible too literally, or treat it too much like a rulebook. It wasn't meant to be this, and it leads to crazy and contradictory conclusions if it is treated this way. Jesus, a masterful rabbinic teacher from 2,000 years ago, did not want people to pluck out their eyes or cut off their hands (Matt. 5:29, 30); He wanted them to understand the importance of the Kingdom of God.

Why do I feel so confident about this? One of the first university courses that I was asked to teach was on the short New Testament letter of St. Paul to the Galatians. I translated the book and read many commentaries and prepared lectures that covered all of the verses in the six chapters. Over the course of my academic career, I think I have taught the content of this letter close to 20 times. There is a great irony hidden within it: Paul is fighting as hard as he can to impress upon the Galatian Christians that coming to God by faith, and developing this relationship through faith, is vastly superior to attempting to do it in human strength by obeying the Jewish laws. And yet, Paul has become the new Moses! Every little word that he says in one of his letters to the fledgling churches of his day has been turned into a new "do" or "don't" by some group throughout history.

Here are some of the things that he says in this letter:

> 21 I do not nullify the grace of God, for if righteousness comes through the Law, then Christ died needlessly (Gal. 2:21).

> 1 You foolish Galatians, who has bewitched you, before whose eyes Jesus Christ was publicly portrayed as crucified? 2 This is the only thing I want to find out from you: did you receive the Spirit by the works of the Law, or by hearing with faith? (Gal. 3:1, 2).

> 4 You have been severed from Christ, you who are seeking to be justified by law; you have fallen from grace. 5 For we through the Spirit, by faith, are waiting for the hope of righteousness. 6 For in Christ Jesus neither circumcision nor uncircumcision means anything, but faith working through love (Gal. 5:4-6).

Paul is using circumcision as a symbol of whether or not everyone needs to obey all of the laws that are within the Bible. He is adamant that people do not have to do this. And yet many of his own comments have become new laws for Christian people. The Bible is not meant to be a rulebook with a list of laws that people must follow; rather, it is a library of books[1] that all bear witness to the reality of encounters that people had with God in their day. As such, it gives a world of information about what God is like and what He cares for, and it acts as a wonderful guide for us even now. We ought not to be sidetracked by small issues of legalism; we are to learn to value the things that God values: justice, mercy and faithfulness. I would also add love since I believe it is the dominant theme throughout the whole message. In the passage above, Paul basically says that nothing means anything except faith working through love.

Not Standing Still

An important thing to realize about proper interpretation of the Bible is the necessity of watching the evolution of the message. Interpretation must be progressive because the message is given in a changing way. God deals with people within their context. I believe that He meets people where they are at.

Here's an example: when the Mosaic Law declared, "eye for eye, tooth for tooth, hand for hand, foot for foot" (Ex. 21:24), it was not meant as a harsh form of judgment. Rather, it was a limitation on tribal warfare and revenge. We can see a story in Genesis 34 where the tribes of Israel rose up against a people whose prince raped Dinah, a daughter of Jacob. In the bloodlust for revenge, her brothers wiped out all of the prince's subjects. In context, "an eye for an eye" is a reasonable and fair punishment. It can prevent a massacre. However, it doesn't go nearly far enough in representing God's heart. Jesus taught people to "turn the other cheek" (Matt. 5:39). He counselled love for enemies and forgiveness for all. He also modelled this.

Another example has to do with the Mosaic Law's exclusion from the Tabernacle of people with crushed testicles and foreigners in the land (Deut 23:1-3). This law is later reversed in Isaiah 56. It is probably not an accident that of the thousands of conversion stories in the early church, one gets special note: the Ethiopian eunuch (Acts 8:25-40). He is even studying the same part of Isaiah. What a beautiful way to demonstrate that the prophetic utterances of Isaiah are coming true as a result of Jesus' life and ministry!

One more example is apparent in Psalm 50. This is where, with poetic images that cause the reader to remember the covenant at Mount Sinai, God explains that He would rather not have all of the animals that the people obediently bring as sacrifices. He asked for them as part of the Mosaic Law. However, since He owns the "cattle on a thousand hills," He would be happy if they just learned to live in honest relationship with Him (Ps. 50:14-15; 23). This part seems quaint, almost like a parent explaining something to a child.

Reaches Beyond Itself

This same idea can be seen in another realm of life, too: slavery. Hidden in the letters of Paul are the seeds of its destruction, but slavery is definitely acceptable to the authors of both the Old and New Testament. So not only is there movement in understanding God's desires within the progressive unfolding of the Biblical message, there are also indications that this is not meant to stop at the end of the writing process. Paul said, "Masters, grant to your slaves justice and fairness, knowing that you too have a Master in heaven" (Col. 4:1). It took many years, almost 1800, before Christian people realized that the implications of such a statement went beyond the words in the Scriptures and demanded action. Against a good deal of resistance, faithful people rose up and campaigned for the freedom of the slaves in Britain, then the British Empire, and people in America and other lands followed suit. There was great resistance to this within the church, though, for many Christians, and many pastors, owned slaves. The Bible was used to defend this practice; people believed that the Bible taught that some races were meant to serve others. As people began to question this and teach against it, there was a great uproar from those who believed that this would mean the abandonment of the Scriptures.[3] The same arguments were heard about a century later as African-Americans were given the vote, and again as schools were integrated.

Can be a Compromise

An important thing to realize is that not all of the Bible teaching represents God's heart. Sometimes it's just a record of how people got things wrong. But even when it's giving precepts and laws about how to live, it can be a compromise between what God wants and what He knows people can accept. At least it seems as though this is what Jesus is saying in Matthew 19 when he discusses divorce and marriage with his friends: "Because of your hardness of heart Moses permitted you to divorce your wives; but from the beginning it has not been this way" (Matt. 19:8).

In other words, God wants people to love each other faithfully and He is against divorce; however, He allowed it to be permitted in the Mosaic Law because He could see that people were not at a place to accept His real standard. This is amazing: even the Bible indicates that not all of the moral and ethical teachings within its pages accurately reflect the heart of God.

I was divorced early in life after about six or seven years of marriage. It was a very sad and difficult time for me, as I'm sure it was for my first wife. It never occurred to me that I could not remarry, because I hadn't been raised in a religiously legalistic way. I thought that the divorce represented a failure on both our parts but that life was big, and that God would want both of us to acknowledge our brokenness and start again. I believed He wanted people to grow and to be happy. A few Christians questioned this attitude but, fortunately, I thought they were crazy. When I met my second wife, the love of my life, I felt free to begin a relationship with her. That was about three decades ago, and we have dedicated our lives to loving God and people together. I think it's fair to say that our four children, and quite a few others besides, are happy that we went forward into life with the belief that God accepted us with all of our mess, loved us completely, and wanted to grow us up into a life of wholeness and maturity. We are still somewhere along that path, but it has been a rich journey.

On the other hand, I have heard at times about churches that have interpreted the Scriptures differently. Believing that theology is God's standard and that people ought to be encouraged to live up to it, they have treated people harshly and insensitively. Somewhere along the way they missed the idea that "mercy triumphs over judgment" (James. 2:13). Instead of bringing God's love to the places of brokenness that people experience, they have insisted on moral standards as though they were laws. Insult gets added to injury as people are not helped, not welcomed, and not embraced by legalistic groups that insist that they know the mind of God. What a travesty. It all has to do with the direction of the ministry: beating people with words to try to get them to reach some pristine standard, or flooding them with love and acceptance so that they are secure enough to begin the process of growth.

It Really is About Love

Jesus reduced all of the Mosaic Law to two principles: loving God and loving people. He went about His life and work including people that everyone else rejected. The only people that Jesus was harsh with were the religious people who felt that they were better than others. To everyone else, commoners, sinners, foreigners, sick people, beggars, political collaborators with a hostile empire, He brought a sense of welcome, inclusion, acceptance and hope.

St. Paul gave a profound description of love in one of his letters (1 Cor. 13). In another he basically said, "nothing means anything except faith working through love" (Gal. 5:6).

And one of the greatest of the church fathers, St. Augustine (d. AD 430), taught that love was essential in interpretation, too. He fought against people who insisted upon literal readings of the creation narratives in Genesis because He felt that this would stop intelligent non-believers of his day from being interested in the rest of the Bible. He wrote,

> When so many meanings, all of them acceptable as true, can be extracted from the words that Moses wrote, do you not see how foolish it is to make a bold assertion that one in particular is the one he had in mind? Do you not see how foolish it is to enter into mischievous arguments which are an offense against that very charity for the sake of which he wrote every one of the words that we are trying to explain?[4]

I am impressed by the irony that he has recognized: it is possible to interpret the message of love in an unloving way. This can be done by insisting that only one interpretation, our own, is the correct one, even when others are just as possible. Another way is to hammer people with laws and words that make them feel the brunt of exclusion. God is not likely to be very happy about either of these.

Clement, an early bishop of Rome, perhaps the third after St. Peter (according to church tradition), wrote a letter to the Corinthians about 40 years after St. Paul had written 1 Corinthians (a likely date is AD 96). It's interesting to compare the letters as they focus on the same themes. Clement also has a stirring passage on love, one of the greatest in Christian literature. And he, too, stands against the insistence that some people have about their ideas being right:

> Self-assertion, self-assurance, and a bold manner are the marks of men accursed of God; it is those who show consideration for others, and are unassuming and quiet, who win His blessing.[5]

Many times people have believed that they were being faithful to God, standing upon the truth, when in reality they were exercising pride in the correctness of their interpretations. Love allows people to listen to others and to accept the possibility that their ideas, too, may have validity. This is in line with what James told us about the kind of wisdom that God values:

> But the wisdom from above is first pure, then peaceable, gentle, reasonable, full of mercy and good fruits, unwavering, without hypocrisy. And

the seed whose fruit is righteousness is sown in peace by those who make peace (James 3:7, 8).

The Power of Worldview

One of the reasons that it's so hard for us to have a new understanding of something is that we see through filters, lenses of our own construction. It's difficult for us to consider things that don't fit within the limitations of our worldview. This seems to be part of the human condition: we need to filter reality because we don't have time in life to make constant decisions about the steady stream of data that is picked up by our senses. However, this can make it very hard for us to have a new thought. Psychological experiments have shown that we feel secure within our filtered systems and we resist anything that threatens to change our way of looking at the world. Physiological signs of stress can accompany our resistance, at times leading towards anger and fear. This helps to explain the amount of time that it can take for someone to change his or her belief about something. An extraordinary example is how difficult it was to persuade doctors to wash their hands after doing autopsies in the 19th century, in spite of the fact that there was an immediate reduction in the mortality rates of their next patients when they were compelled to do so.[6]

I'm convinced that resistance to change is valuable. If we weren't slow to adapt we might be far too flighty, going off in many directions without a solid foundation for our beliefs and values. Resistance, too, presses against new ideas and forces them to be well articulated and well developed. But, of course, resistance can be too strong and can get in the way of a new way of seeing, even if it is an improvement upon an older way.

Some people are early adaptors to change, some follow after a time, some follow with great reluctance, and some are adamantly against change of any sort.

One of the times that the prophet Jeremiah was complaining to God about the difficulty of his calling in life, bringing a message to people that they did not want to hear, God answered in this way:

> If you will return then I will restore you; before Me you will stand. And if you can extract the precious from the worthless, then you will be My spokesman (Jer. 15:19).

An essential skill in sorting through the precious and the worthless in any area of life is what I've started calling a teleological suspension of disbelief. I thought I had taken this term from Soren Kierkegaard (he spoke of a "teleological suspension of the ethical" in *Fear and Trembling* as he discussed Abraham's willingness to sacrifice Isaac)[7] but perhaps I stumbled into using it without realizing that it was something new. In any event, it seems to help people understand the concept, so I'll share it here.

While we are listening to someone who has a contrary viewpoint, we are often formulating our next argument. This is not listening! This is defense of a worldview. The word 'teleological' comes from the Greek word, *teleios*, meaning "end" or "goal." The phrase, therefore, means a purposeful suspension of disbelief. For a good reason or purpose, we take our own thoughts and beliefs and lay them gently on the back burner of our mental stoves. We do this so that we can really hear what someone else is saying. And we do it so that we can entertain the possibility that we might be able to learn something from a different point of view. Once we have heard them with innocent ears, we can return to our own ideas and see how they agree or disagree. Often a synthesis is possible. This skill, combined with accurate empathy, allows us to begin to imagine the world in the way that the other person sees it. This is what is necessary for real encounter. Otherwise all we have is a battle of words falling against defensive walls. We think we have understood an opposing argument, but really all we know is the shell of the idea; we have not experienced it from the inside. Only from that vantage point is it possible to begin to allow the seeds of a new idea to grow and perhaps challenge our own thought fortresses.

The negative side of this equation has been clearly taught by Jesuit priest and psychotherapist, Anthony de Mello:

> You see persons and things not as they are but as you are. If you wish to see them as they are you must attend to your attachments and the fears that your attachments generate. Because when you look at life it is these attachments and fears that will decide what you will notice and what you block out. Whatever you notice then commands your attention. And since your looking has been selective you have an illusory version of the things and people around you. The more you live with this distorted version the more you become convinced that it is the only true picture of the world because your attachments and fears continue to process incoming data in a way that will reinforce your picture.[8]

But there is a better way. Jesus taught us to love in the way that we would like to be loved (Matt. 7:12). We call this the Golden Rule. In the last century, Hasidic Rabbi and professor of philosophy, Martin Buber, reframed this by depicting I-it and I-Thou relations. He suggested that I-it is a default position that allows me to use the people that I meet for my own ends; they remain as objects to me. I-Thou demands that I attribute the same value of subject-hood to the person I encounter as I claim for myself.[9] When we speak, particularly about matters of ultimate concern, we all want to be heard. Learning to truly listen is part of what it means to learn to love; it is also an essential aspect of maturity.

Searching for the Beautiful Answer

There is a verse in the New Testament that I believe holds an important secret for those who value the idea of becoming like Christ:

> But solid food is for the mature, who because of practice have their senses trained to discern good and evil (Heb. 5:14).

The word used here for "mature" comes from *teleios*, the same word that gave us the sense of purpose or goal. As a side note, it might have been better to translate this word in a way that was closer to its root meaning in the Sermon on the Mount. In English it often reads:

> Therefore you are to be perfect, as your heavenly Father is perfect (Matt 5:48).

The idea that we need to be perfect in the same way

that God is perfect can be quite discouraging and it's unnecessary. Why not translate it something like this:

> Therefore you should grow toward your goal in the same way that your heavenly Father reflects His ...

or,

> Therefore you should be mature as your heavenly Father is mature ...

Translators might have been offended at the notion that there is change in God. I can see why they would want to steer away from this. However, in order to protect their theological assumption they have stacked the moral cards quite heavily against the poor people who have to try reach for a perfection they can never attain.

I should return to my main point, though. Hebrews 5:14 mentions a group of people called "mature ones" and it says that they got that way through daily practice. The thing that characterizes them as mature is that they have the ability to discern between good and evil. Here's where the secret lies. The Greek word for "good" that we would expect, *agathos*, is not used here. Neither is the word, *agathosuné*, which is the word that is listed in the fruit of the Spirit passage in Galatians 5:22. Both of these have strong overtones of moral goodness. Instead, the word *kalos* is used. This word does mean "good" but it has a rich connotation of beauty. A vase might have been called *kalos* if it was beautifully made. I don't want to overdo this point because words in ancient Greek are used somewhat interchangeably, just as they are in any language, but I find one implication compelling. Perhaps maturity is really about seeing past a good answer in order to find a beautiful one.

If a parent forces a child to obey in a certain situation the outcome may be good. If the parent creates an environment where the child chooses for him or herself it's closer to beauty. If a pastor hammers at people to read their Bibles or to do some good work, it may be good. If an environment allows people to grow up into a desire to be faithful and kind, or to do some good thing, it's definitely better.

When Joseph learned that Mary, the mother of Jesus, was pregnant before he had slept with her, he was forced with a dilemma. How should he respond? The text says this:

> And Joseph her husband, being a righteous man and not wanting to disgrace her, planned to send her away secretly (Matt. 1:19).

Apparently, there is more than one way to be righteous in the eyes of God. A righteous response according to law would have been to expose her shame to the community as a preface to execution in most situations (Deut. 22:13-29). Joseph, instead, offered mercy. For this, for ignoring the law in order to care for a person, he is called righteous. He also shows himself to be a fit role model for the Child that Mary is bearing—Jesus will make similar decisions again and again. Perhaps, in the context of the day, following the law would have been *agathos*. Joseph did something *kalos*, beautiful.

Reaching for a Conclusion

Gregory the Great (AD 540-604) is remembered as one of the best of the popes. He was a gifted administrator and spiritual director, known for character and generosity. Soon after he was selected as pope, even though it was against his will, he embraced the role and wrote a book called *Pastoral Care*. It became the main text for preparing pastors for more than 1,000 years. Near the beginning he offers this piece of wisdom:

> No one ventures to teach any art unless he has learned it after deep thought. With what rashness, then, would the pastoral office be undertaken by the unfit, seeing that the government of souls is the art of arts! For who does not realize that the wounds of the mind are more hidden than the internal wounds of the body?[10]

I think he was right. The governance of souls is an art. And so is proper biblical interpretation. There are many contradictory ideas in the 66 books of our Bibles. We are told not to judge (Matt. 7:1) and we are also warned to beware of false prophets (Matt. 7:15). We are told not to let anyone see our good deeds (Matt. 6:1), and we are told to "let them shine" (Matt. 5:16). What principles govern when to do what?

Personally, I am glad that the Bible is not a rulebook. What it offers is far better. Within its pages people can learn about God and can meet with God. They can have their hearts broken for the poor and for their own failures, and they can be built into people who freely love others. The Bible provides an atmosphere that helps us change and grow. But it does not do this if we remain locked within a childish perspective of trying to obey its every whim. Instead, we are meant to become mature as we go through life. Learning from those who have gone before, we learn to balance the messages and see the thing to do that has the chance of bringing a beautiful result.

Thomas Oden said it this way:

> The fabric of effective pastoral work involves the constant interweaving of scriptural wisdom, historical awareness, constructive theological reasoning, situational discernment, and personal empathy.[11]

Howard Stone and James Duke, in *How to Think Theologically*, teach that there is a difference between "embedded" and "deliberative" theology.[12] Embedded thought is picked up naturally as we go through life; it involves the answers we've been given and have often accepted without too many questions. Deliberative theology is different; it's what we choose after we've given a matter a good deal of thought. A student of mine was delighted to notice that "deliberative" contains the root of the word "liberate." Hopefully, liberation and freedom will be the results of deeper reflection based upon study and experience.

Stone and Duke say that we have theological worldviews that control or filter what we believe about ideas that relate to God and how to live for Him. They write:

> Perhaps the easiest way to recognize the key to a theologian's template or to discover your own embedded theological template is to look for what is emphasized. Every theologian operates with a certain set of core theological views—favored images, categories, and themes. These primary theological views stand in the foreground, against a backdrop of the theologian's other, less central notions. Or, changing our metaphor to music, we might liken the key ingredients in the makeup of a theological template to

melody lines: less crucial elements are the notes of harmony or counterpoint.[13]

I came to realize the truth of this for myself when I pondered all the ways that I had interpreted the ancient story of Cain and Abel (Gen. 4:1-16). As a young Christian, I had been told that Abel's sacrifice was acceptable to God because it involved blood (apparently this was necessary to satisfy God in some way). Later, as I grew away from fundamentalist groups and studied at evangelical seminaries, I was told that Abel's sacrifice was accepted because he brought God his best. Years later, when I began to have experiences with God that charismatic Christians talk about, I saw Cain as jealous that he didn't have the same mystical experience with God that Abel had (his "countenance" went down instead of up). When my interest moved toward counselling and inner healing, I noted Cain's skill at deflecting blame from himself. Later, when I began to think more about issues of justice, I learned from listening to a friend that the story is about God's care for the marginalized: Cain has all the advantages (see how his mother speaks of him) but God is close to the forgotten poor.

Brian McLaren must be right when he teaches that not only do we read the Bible; it, in fact, reads us.[14] The emphasis we give the text shows a great deal about our theological template and about where we are coming from. If we focus on the text thinking that it is the legal requirement of a demanding God, we will see it one way. If we see it as a series of stories that invite us in to meet with God ourselves, we will see it another. If we see it in this last way, and believe that God is love, and desire to be changed by encounters with Him until we begin to reflect His character, it becomes all the richer.

And many interpreters have believed something like this. In *Pirke Aboth, Chapters of the Fathers*, there is a collection of ethical teachings from ancient Judaism. One of the writers, Rabbi Chanina ben Dosa, who was a contemporary of Jesus and considered one of the best men of his time, said,

> If your concern for others exceeds your desire for wisdom, your wisdom will endure. If your desire for wisdom exceeds your concern for others, your wisdom will not endure ... If your kindness exceeds your wisdom, your wisdom will endure. If your wisdom exceeds your kindness, your wisdom will not endure.[15]

Then this is recorded, from the same man,

> If you bring joy to others, God rejoices in you. If you bring no joy to others, God does not rejoice in you.[16]

I have witnessed so many people through the years who meant well but who said things to others that unkindly reflected their own theological template. I know from experience that this does not bring joy.

The great task, it seems to me, is to reach, in a deliberative way, beyond embedded ways of thinking so that we can seek the kindest and most beautiful direction in any given situation. In the final analysis, we need to learn to interpret toward love.

What Difference?

How does all of this affect the question of whether or not to include people of different sexuality in our churches and communities? I once heard Lewis Smedes, in a video presentation before his death in 2002, saying,

> *People have to do the best they can with what they have been given.*[17]

I think he's right. If our interpretation is not limited by law or embedded thinking, it becomes clear that we need to bring God's love to *all* people. Rather than beating people with our sense of how they must change, we need to welcome, embrace, and form community with people so that they can enrich our lives and we, hopefully, can enrich theirs.

For a long time, people thought of homosexuality as a choice. Now, although there is still not complete clarity about why some people are same-gender attracted, it is evident that orientation is not a choice. Some people, very much against their will, are only ever attracted to people of their own gender. What people do as a result of orientation does involve choice, but not the way they feel. The best treatment of this topic that I have found is Justin Lee's book, *Torn: Rescuing the Gospel from the Gays—vs.—Christians Debate*. I recommend this book to anyone interested in this topic. Lee grew up as a serious Southern Baptist who is horrified to realize that he is different from other boys. In his determination to steward his sexuality in a way that pleases God, he endures masses of insensitivity and prejudice from many Christians. He also uncovers many myths that are propagated in Christian circles such as family system stereotypes and heroic examples of orientation change. Studied over a long period, many of these have reverted.[18]

Chapter Three
And What Does the Bible Say?

I hope that I have demonstrated that our interpretations are governed by the emphases we find in the text, and that kindness and beauty and love are better goals than a legalistic sense of morality. And yet I do think it is reasonable to ask what the Bible actually does have to say about homosexuality.

Before I concentrated on trying to understand this topic from a biblical point of view, I assumed, along with everyone else I knew, that the Bible presented a coherent and unified rejection of homosexuality. Now I don't think that this is true. Instead, I think that it's possible that the Bible offers a coherent and unified rejection of certain kinds of homosexuality. My suspicion is that these forms would include: gang rape, idolatrous sexual practices, pederasty, promiscuity, and heterosexual people pushing past their innate sense of right and wrong in the pursuit of sexual pleasure or degradation. A couple of these forms are characterized by domination of a stronger party over a weaker one; others are characterized by departing from a true and beautiful standard set by God in worship, or by going against natural inclination.

But what if the people who gave the very few mentions in the Bible of homosexuality were thinking of its negative aspects and not thinking at all about the minority of people in all societies who find that their orientation and attraction is for their own gender? This seems more and more likely to me.

Just as it's possible that people who lived in ancient times couldn't imagine a world without slavery, so it is possible that the same people couldn't have imagined a more nuanced approach to sexual minorities. With the issue of slavery, as already noted, ideas and principles are given in the Scripture that do lead, over time (a great deal of time) to a more just treatment of people. What if it's the same with different sexuality? Jesus meets many people who are rejected by their societies and He welcomes them into open and honest discourse. He speaks with women of dubious character, with foreigners, with people who are so sick that their society believes them to be cursed by God and untouchable, with political collaborators, with commoners—Jesus consistently treats people, especially the poor and marginalized, with dignity, justice, and compassion. He breaks His own laws in order to do this (examine, for instance, Lev. 13:45-46 and Num. 5:1-4; then look at Lev. 5:1-2—it is unlawful for Jesus to touch lepers).

There is one case where Jesus seems a little hard on a person who comes to Him in need. This is the Syro-Phoenician woman, described in Matthew 15 and Mark 7. I have come to value this story very much. Perhaps Jesus is reflecting the prejudices of His age, but I doubt it. Instead, I think it's more likely that He is saying out loud, either for her sake, or for the disciples who are watching, what everyone believes. He is bringing the hidden darkness into the light of day by speaking openly and honestly about the broken relations between Jews and Gentiles. He is naming the curse. And then He shatters it, both by honouring the woman and by healing her daughter.

What does Jesus have to say about homosexuality? I think that by now everyone knows: absolutely nothing.

But look at how He treats everyone else. He doesn't pick on people who are different and feel broken and isolated. He meets people in their need and accepts them as though they were equals. It could even be said that He treats people as though He is their servant. In spite of exhaustion, He keeps ministering to the crowds of people who find Him wherever He goes. This reminds me of a line from Martin Luther:

> A Christian is a perfectly free lord of all, subject to none. A Christian is a perfectly dutiful servant of all, subject to all.[1]

I know already that some will want to object: "But when He spoke to the woman caught in adultery, He told her to 'Go your way, and sin no more.'" This point is valid. Jesus didn't only accept people; He also gave them a path to a better future. He redeemed, He encouraged, He inspired, and He promised the help of the Holy Spirit to lead people forward into life.

But where exactly is the sin in learning as you grow up that your feelings and attractions are drawn toward people of your own gender? I certainly believe that sinful choices could come from this, just as they could for people whose attractions are for the opposite gender. Let's be clear: it is not a sin to openly acknowledge the truth of what is felt. Orientation is not a sin. Neither is it a choice for many people (I can think of a situation where it might be a choice, but I'd like to discuss that when I begin to describe what I think specific references in the Bible are actually saying).

Remember the verse from Jeremiah 15:19: "And if you extract the precious from the worthless, you will become My spokesman." The great task for us today is to "rightly divide the word of truth" (2 Tim. 2:15, KJV). In my writing about slavery I have noted that there was an acceptance of this evil practice in the Bible at the same time as there was a thrust toward just and compassionate care of others. The two need to be separated or divided from each other. The "worthless" in this case is obvious; the "precious" is the understanding of Jesus's Golden Rule (Matt. 7:12) that gradually leads to equality.

This can be seen in another instance, too. I have already given the Bible's declaration that God is not for divorce. As a divorced man, I am perfectly at peace with that. The Bible is also not for feelings of lust or hatred or violence. I've experienced these, too. I'm at peace with God not liking them. I don't like them myself. But I don't feel as though I have disqualified myself from living a good and full and decent life because I have felt these things. Rather, I acknowledge them as deficits (sins) and move on, asking for God's help to change and grow. And, wonderfully, growth is possible. If I didn't have the standard, I wouldn't know. If I thought the standard was a judgment, I might think that I had to live the rest of my life in some sort of prison.

Divorce is interesting for another reason, too. Over the centuries, many people have taught that it disqualified people from remarriage. But there was an exception clause given in Matthew 5:32 and repeated in Matthew 19:9: "except in cases of adultery" (the Greek word implies sexual misconduct: *porneia*). How do you balance that against the Golden Rule?

What happens if a spouse is abusive and yet has not committed adultery? If you think of the Bible as a rulebook, you can find yourself in the strange position of hoping that the mean-spirited spouse will go out and have sex with someone! I have spoken with pastors who have admitted that this thought has crossed their minds.

But the Bible is not a rulebook. It is an introduction to the wisdom of God, in order that people who love it and treat it with deep respect will become wise themselves.

I remember the first time I found myself counselling a woman to leave a husband who treated her badly even though he had not been sexually unfaithful to her. I could not, and do not, believe that God wanted her to stay in a relationship where she was dominated and dehumanized. How can that be related to treating others as we would like to be treated? Going out past the clear prescription of the Bible felt a little strange, like walking on thin ice, but there was no sense that anything less was in line with God's wisdom and truth. I had to go there. Many others have as well. To pastor means to have the real and best interest of the people at heart, and to work for their good in all situations.

Some legalistic pastors just adjust the boundary: if she is physically abused, she can leave. It's important to note that this is not what the Bible says. It's a compromise with what the pastor sees as necessary in light of justice and wisdom. Of course, some pastors haven't even arrived at this point ....

It's not good enough. A legalistic approach is a failure to walk into the wisdom of God. It is a form of clinging to the Bible without being changed by the Bible.

And yet resistance to change is so strong, that translation teams will even go to fairly great lengths in order to support their way of seeing issues like these. I was shocked to see the translation that one group gave to 1 Corinthians 7: 27 & the first part of v. 28:

> Are you married? Then don't get a divorce. Are you single? Then don't look for a wife. But if you get married, you have not sinned (New International Readers Version).

Paul is telling people that in light of the difficult times, he thinks it's best for them to stay in whatever condition they find themselves. But he wants to let them know that life happens, and he understands that, and not every situation fits nicely in a rule. So he tells them that if they do marry, they have not sinned.

My issue is that the verse reads quite differently in Greek than it does in this particular English translation. The first word that beginning Greek students used to learn was *luo* "to loose" or "destroy." It is in both parts of verse 27. Here's another translation (NASB):

Are you bound to a wife? Do not seek to be released. Are you released from a wife? Do not seek a wife. But if you marry, you have not sinned ...

This is a good and fair translation. Whatever is being described in the first clause is also true for the second. "Do not seek the *luo* of your marriage; if your marriage has had a *luo*, don't make it the aim of your life to get married again. However, if it happens, you haven't sinned ...." Please note, the first translation above is not being fair when it implies that it's ok for single people to get married. That is not what the verse says. It is talking about people who have had a marriage implode.

Here's the irony: even if you treated the Bible as a rulebook, it would have been kinder to you than many parts of the church.

And, for all of the reasons that I have given in these pages, it is important not to treat the Bible as a rulebook.

Specific References to Homosexuality

There have been many fine discussions in recent times of the seven passages in Scripture that speak of homosexuality. Some go into much greater depth than I will here. A good treatment is found in *Jesus, the Bible, and Homosexuality* by Jack Rogers (he also looks at an eighth passage, Jude, verses 5-8, but this is so obscure that most people don't include it in the discussion—I've decided to leave it out). But any treatment ought to begin by noting that seven references, and none from Jesus, ensures that this is a minor theme. There are hundreds, if not thousands, of verses that relate to economic oppression of the poor or greed and selfishness.

Genesis 19 and Judges 19

Two early references are clearly against the mob violence of gang rape that violates the ancient duty of hospitality. The mobs in question are running wild, wanting to dominate strangers in a way that demonstrates how powerful they are: by treating men as though they were women in a society where women were often seen as property.[2] These passages have nothing to do with loving and faithful homosexual unions. Since one of them, Genesis 19, has to do with the story of Sodom and Gomorrah, there has been a remembrance of this ever after in the word "sodomy." Sodom is almost analogous with homosexuality in the thinking of some people. Much later in the Bible, though, the prophet Ezekiel referred to the lands of Israel and Judah in his day as being like Sodom and Gomorrah. He defined the sin of Sodom in a way that is instructive for all ages:

49 Behold, this was the guilt of your sister Sodom: she and her daughters had arrogance, abundant food and careless ease, but she did not help the poor and needy. 50 Thus they were haughty and committed abominations before Me. Therefore I removed them when I saw it (Ezek. 16:49-50).

If one idea in this passage (arrogant abundance that ignored the plight of the poor) can be seen to represent the root of the problem, and another (whatever abominations were done) can be seen as symptomatic, it's possible that traditional elements in our societies have been attacking the wrong enemy.

Leviticus 18 and 20

Another two references to homosexuality in the Old Testament are part of a Holiness Code of behaviours that ancient Israelites found necessary in order for them to survive in a hostile environment. Personally, I believe that these commands came to them from God, but I have already indicated that laws like these are sometimes a compromise between what God wants for the people and what He knows they can accept (remember Matthew 19 regarding divorce). They may also have been necessary for the maintenance of these patriarchal tribes. An excellent description of patriarchal life as it relates to understanding the Old Testament is given in Sandra Richter's *The Epic of Eden*. So many ancient stories begin to make more sense when this background is in place.[3]

One of God's main concerns in this part of the Old Testament is to help His people understand that the moralities of the ancient Egyptians (where they were slaves) and those of the ancient Canaanites (whose land they were set to invade) were not yet in line with His desires. He wanted something better, kinder, more just, and more gracious for His people. In fact, it seems as though He begins His dealings with the Israelites by setting boundaries of exclusion that He will later soften, just as soon as they learn something about His nature and will. This seems very much like parenting to me: "Don't play in the road!" will become "Hold Mommy's hand while we cross the street." Finally, it will be something like: "Remember to fill-up the gas tank before you come home!" God's love looks as though it is only for the Israelites until they are grown up enough to hear that He actually loves all the peoples:

> "Are you not as the sons of Ethiopia to Me, O sons of Israel?" declares the Lord. "Have I not brought up Israel from the land of Egypt, And the Philistines from Caphtor and the Arameans from Kir?" (Amos 9:7)

Sometimes people are still being childish as they read the Bible and think that God loves only Israel, or that the Israelites have such a special place in His heart that He assists them in ruthless treatment and domination of other lands. Sometimes people transfer this kind of special relationship to their own nationalities and think that God is "for" them in a way that He is not for others. There are various ways of rationalizing this kind of belief system, but it has nothing to do with a mature relationship with the living God of the Bible.

I think there is a way that God does "play favourites" but it has nothing to do with political systems. Rather, it's for those who whole-heartedly wish to do His will in the world. There are quite a few passages that support this idea:

> ... those who honor Me I will honor, and those who despise Me will be lightly esteemed (1 Samuel 2:30).

> ... the Lord is with you when you are with Him. And if you seek Him, He will let you find Him; but if you forsake Him, He will forsake you (2 Chronicles 15:2).

> For the eyes of the Lord move to and fro throughout the earth that He may strongly support those whose heart is completely His (2 Chronicles 16:9).

Draw near to God and He will draw near to you (James 4:8).

But, back to the main idea! It is widely known that there are two passages in the Levitical Holiness Code that speak of "lying with a man as with a woman" as an abomination (Lev. 18:22; 20:13). A good deal of cultural background is probably necessary in order to understand what is being said here. The Hebrew word being used for "abomination" is *toevah*. At this time of history it may be related to a sense of ritual uncleanness,[4] and it and other words that are given the same translation in English are declared for quite a few other things as well. Some of them leave us puzzled because they don't seem so bad to us today. One of the reasons for this is that they were not meant for us in the same way that they were meant for these ancient Israelites. For us, there are insights into the holiness of God—these are forever. But for them, there are specifics about how to reflect that holiness in a way that helped them to survive as a patriarchal society. They have strong prohibitions on wearing garments made of more than one material or sowing more than one kind of seed in a field. Perhaps this is to keep them focused on the need for purity.[5] We don't know. But many things in the Old Testament are called an abomination. Here is a short list aside from some of the sexual ones in the Levitical Holiness Code:

- Pride (Prov. 6:16-19)
- Lying (Prov. 6:16-19)
- Being a false witness (Prov. 6:16-19)
- Violent shedding of innocent blood (Prov. 6:16-19)
- Spreading strife among brothers (Prov. 6:16-19)
- A false balance in business deals (Prov. 11:1)
- Justifying the wicked and condemning the righteous (Prov. 17:15)
- Wearing clothing from the opposite gender (Deut. 22:5)
- Acting unjustly (Deut. 25:16)
- Offering worship when you don't care for the poor or live justly (Isaiah 1:10-23)
- Idolatry (Ezek. 18:5-13, and many other places)
- Adultery (Ezek. 18:5-13)
- Oppressing the poor and needy (Ezek. 18:5-13)
- Having intercourse with a woman during her menstrual period (Ezek. 18:5-13)
- Lending money at interest (Ezek. 18:5-13)
- Eating lobster and other shellfish (Lev. 11:10)

When we see it like this, a few things are obvious: first, we are all involved in societies that would be labelled "abomination" by the standards of God's early dealings with the Israelites; second, we have all been involved in activities that ought to be labeled this way; third, it's not fair to pick out one (homosexuality, for instance) and treat it as worse than the rest; fourth, some of the specific Israelite prohibitions were for their society and not for ours—we live in a different cultural context. Regarding this last point, it's not that we can't learn from each of these things; it's that they are not all directly relatable in the same way. Our society's economy is built upon lending at interest. We live in a different time. Perhaps this was even different by Jesus's day, for He uses interest as a positive notion in one of His parables (Matt. 25:14-27). We should learn from the wisdom of the past in order to make wise decisions about righteousness in our own day.

1 Corinthians 6:9 & 1 Timothy 1:10

There are clear prohibitions of homosexuality in the English New Testament, but the Greek word that is used is quite obscure. It's hard to know exactly what is meant. Both of the passages above list behaviours that disqualify people from "inheriting the kingdom of God." The Greek word *arsenokoites* is part of both lists. It has been translated "homosexuality" or something like it in recent years. When I checked with older Bibles it is sometimes translated as "sodomites," or as "those who defile themselves with men." Jack Rogers quotes various scholars who think that this word, coming from *arsen* (male) and *koites* (bed) is not a clear-cut ancient term for homosexuality. It may have referred instead to some form of commercial sexual exploitation.[6] Others have wondered if it refers to a specific sexual act or to forms of idolatrous worship. There are about 70 usages of this term in ancient writings after the NT, but almost all of them are lists of sins. Of the ones that aren't, it seems that at least one refers to an act men carry out with their wives.[7] If some in the ancient world saw this as a sexual sin that could also be heterosexual, how can we be certain that it ought to be translated "homosexuality"? We do not know for sure what this word meant.

Can it possibly be right to condemn a whole segment of people, even if they are a minority (I'm trying to be ironic here), to celibacy and enforced loneliness on the basis of an obscure term?

Of course, it is my contention that even if we knew that the word stood for homosexuality we would not know whether or not that meant all forms or only perverse or debased forms. It might have nothing at all to do, in the mind of the writer, with faithful and loving committed relationships. And, even if it did, the Bible is the place we go to meet God and to become wise, not to be reined in with rules on every side.

Romans 1: 18-32

In my understanding of the New Testament, one passage stood above all others in keeping me from a full acceptance of homosexual union—Romans 1: 26-27. Here it is:

> 26 For this reason God gave them over to degrading passions; for their women exchanged the natural function for that which is unnatural, 27 and in the same way also the men abandoned the natural function of the woman and burned in their desire toward one another, men with men committing indecent acts and receiving in their own persons the due penalty of their error.

Some of the Old Testament passages had to do with violence and domination; others had to do with tribal purity behaviours that seemed, at least in part, quite disconnected from the way we live today. The only mention of homosexuality in the New Testament aside from Romans 1 are the lists I've just described, and it's hard to know exactly what was being referred to in those lists. But Romans 1 seemed as clear as could be—God does not like this behaviour.

Some scholars have suggested that we don't know everything that forms the cultural context of the passage. Perhaps it is describing practices that were part of idolatrous worship carried on by non-Jewish nations.[8] That would make sense as the passage is clearly about worship of the true God versus idolatrous worship of things that God has made (Rom. 1:25).

However, I think the meaning is a little different than this. To understand it, I think it's important to keep the whole passage in mind. Paul is forming an argument about the universal need for relationship with God by faith in Christ. He is going to focus first on the need of the Gentile nations and then he will turn his attention to the need of the Jewish people. His point is that both are far from God and that nothing has worked to bring them closer. The Gentiles have worshipped the wrong things and have gradually fallen into worse and worse behaviours. The Jews are full of pride at their special status with God and the fact that they have the Scriptures, but their life is often off track, too. In fact, Paul's sense is that everyone has fallen short of the image of God and it's wrong to judge others. Since we're all part of broken systems, we don't have that right. Wonderfully, God has provided a new way (though it was promised long before): faith in Jesus Christ. This provides direct access to a loving relationship with God for all people that is not related to a level of behaviour or morality. All people are accepted as they receive a gift that is freely offered to them.

The first part of the argument, Romans 1:18-32, seems specifically focused on Gentile nations who carried on many behaviours that were considered abysmal by the Jews (including their dietary practices). Paul speaks about a downward spiral of behaviour that flows from worshipping the wrong things. He uses the phrase, "God gave them over ...," three different times, each one seeming worse than the last. Since they didn't worship properly, God gave them over to a loosened moral standard. As time went on, God gave them over to an abnormal moral standard. Finally, He gave them over to the worst thing of all, a depraved mind. Life from this place is almost entirely backwards, with people applauding immoral behaviour. It's like they've lost a proper view of reality and see everything through a darkened lens. Envy and murder and strife are mentioned, along with deceit and jealousy and pride. Other characteristics include greed, gossip, and disobedience to parents. And then, worst of all, the list concludes with one word: unmerciful.

The place where homosexuality is found is in the second step, that of an abnormal moral standard. This is translated in some versions as "degrading passions" (NRSV, NASB) or "dishonorable passions" (NET) or "vile passions" (NKJV). The point of the flow of the argument, though, is that things are getting worse. Not connected to a proper focus of worship, people do not have a healthy place to fix their loyalty and devotion outside of themselves. This changes everything. Gradually their behaviour begins to mirror the notions that they do hold dear. Standards fall off in the first instance of the "God gave them over ..." phrase. In the second, people are pushing beyond intuitive barriers, pressing toward more and more outrageous behaviours. They are experimenting sexually and pushing past the place that feels natural to them in order to try for more and more sensual satisfaction. This is what is being depicted here. In the third instance of the phrase, people end up completely backwards, living with the results and consequences of following a bad direction. They are spiritually blind and unable to see the way back to a better view on reality and life.

The next chapter will begin with a rebuke for all who judge others (Rom. 2:1) because it is Paul's conviction that everyone is somewhere along this broken spectrum. Unmerciful judging will actually prove that it is so. The Jews might complain that they are in a more exalted moral position, but Paul will use the rest of the chapter to show the impartial nature of God's (more honest) judgment, and then he will remind them of various forms of hypocrisy that they have committed. They, too, are part of the downward spiral.

I am now convinced that the homosexuality that Paul is writing about is of the nature that I've described above. It refers to heterosexual people who are pressing past their intuitive sexual orientation in order to strive for greater and greater sensual experience.[9]

It has nothing to do with the minority of people who find that they have always and only been oriented toward their own gender, or toward those who realize that they are same-gender attracted as their sexuality matures. This, like a world free of slavery, is an understanding too nuanced for a message that was produced two thousand years ago. We gain understanding as we go.

If anyone doubts that some people are actually oriented toward their own gender, they owe it to themselves to read a book I mentioned earlier, Justin Lee's *Torn: Rescuing the Gospel from the Gays—Vs.— Christians Debate*. I think it is impossible to maintain the idea that homosexual orientation is a choice after honest and thoughtful reflection based on this book. My belief, based on the passage I have just described, is that homosexual choice is a possibility for some who are trying to press out of naturally felt boundaries.[10] For others, like Lee, or for the many examples of people he describes who tried unsuccessfully to heal their orientation through various forms of reparative therapy, it most certainly is not.

Another Take

I recently learned about a thoughtful message given on this passage by Matt Croasmun, a pastor in New Haven, Connecticut. It fits well with what I've said above but adds one element to explain it even further. He suggests that the historical situation of Romans plays a role in its meaning.[11] I will take his ideas and weave in a little background knowledge to illustrate them. We know from the historian Suetonius that Jews had been expelled from Rome in AD 51 for arguing over someone named "Chrestus." Scholars believe that Suetonius misunderstood the name—it makes sense that Jews and Gentiles would have been arguing over "Christus." Paul probably wrote Romans five or six years later. By this time Jewish people were gradually finding their way back into the city. And some of them believed in Jesus. But as they came they were reintroducing parts of the old argument: they felt a sense of moral superiority over the Gentiles who had entered the church. Therefore, Paul starts a brilliant piece of rhetoric in a way that would draw them in: he describes the characteristic sins of the Gentile nations in a way that the Jewish believers would applaud. But then he lowers the boom by pointing out that they are just as bad in the ways that I've already described.

There is historic precedent for this technique. The prophet Amos used it after the northern kingdom of

Israel was separated from the southern kingdom of Judah. He came from the south and wanted to bring a message from God to the people in the north. He caught their attention by describing the sins of the surrounding nations, and then he focused on the sins of Judah, his own land. People must have been feeling that he was the most enlightened prophet in history. That's when he directed his attention, finally, on the sins of Israel, the northern kingdom. And the rest of the book is a scathing rebuke of *their* societal injustices.

Later in history, Bernard of Clairvaux did a similar thing. He brought a message of moderation to the monks at Cluny because of their luxurious lifestyle. However, he focused first on the problems of spiritual pride that he saw in his own Cistercian movement.

If Croasmun is right, Paul is describing Gentile culture in exactly the way the Jews would have seen it: full of idolatry and indiscriminate sexual practices, as well as all the other examples of bad character that are sometimes experienced in human societies. Then, in Chapter 2, he shines the light on their own hypocrisy and sinfulness as they pretend to live at a higher level. The stage has been set with eloquence and brilliance for the equalizing statements in Chapter 3. All have sinned and fallen short of God's glory; all need the salvation that comes by faith in Christ. The added implication hangs over the argument: no one should be lording anything over anyone else. No one should reject or exclude people based on a supposed sense of moral superiority.

How would these ideas affect the argument that I've made about Romans 1 describing heterosexuals who are pushing past natural boundaries? I think these perspectives fit well together. Croasmun's idea is that Paul is shining a light on sins the Jews considered characteristic of Gentile life, with idolatry and sexual immorality topping the list. He is doing this to draw in the Jewish members of the audience. There is nothing being said here that relates to loving and faithful unions among the minority of people around the world who are same-gender attracted. That was not the focus or intent of this passage. Given the worldviews and assumptions of ancient societies, it may not even have been possible for people to entertain such a thought.

Summing Up

Learning to interpret toward love is the best orientation for those who value, honour, and respect the inspiration of the Bible. Other templates of belief are possible, but it is only this one that is in line with the nature of the Divine Author behind the many human authors of the text. He is described as Love (1 Jn. 4:18). His ways are merciful. When Jesus walks among us to show us what the Father is like, He embraces the forgotten, lonely and rejected. He shows compassion to outsiders. He does tell people to "go and sin no more," but there is no clear evidence from the Bible that loving, faithful, committed homosexual unions are sinful. Even if there was such evidence, I would argue that the Bible is not a collection of rules that we are meant to mindlessly follow. Paul speaks more clearly and forcefully about the need for women to wear head-coverings than he does about homosexuality. Time after time representatives of the church have tried to hold on to traditional understandings that were later acknowledged by almost all to be obstacles to just and compassionate treatment of others. I think we are in a long process of being set free from such thinking. In the Scriptures we get to meet with and be transformed by the One who is Love. We learn to think for ourselves, and to reach beyond the smallness of conventional moralities that advantage and privilege majorities. We learn to see the ultimate concerns of others as important, too. In fact, to have an ever-increasing sense of value for wider and wider circles of people is probably the key characteristic hidden in our understanding of what maturity looks like. This is the teaching of the Christian developmental psychologist, James Fowler,[12] who gave us many studies on stages of faith, and it is in line with Buber's *I and Thou* and with the Golden

Rule of Jesus. He taught us to love even our enemies. All of these perspectives converge on the importance of treating the other in the way that we would like to be treated.

N. T. Wright has written that the Bible presents a kind of five-act drama as it moves through creation, fall, Israel, Jesus and the church. He says,

> We must act in the appropriate manner for *this* moment in the story; this will be in direct continuity with the previous acts (we are not free to jump suddenly to another narrative, a different play altogether), but such continuity also implies discontinuity, a moment where genuinely new things can and do happen. We must be ferociously loyal to what has gone before and cheerfully open about what must come next.[13]

Another way that he teaches about this is found in his illustration of a ship to a new world:

> It is not hard to imagine illustrations of how this continuity and discontinuity function. When travelers sail across a vast ocean and finally arrive on the distant shore, they leave the ship behind and continue over land, not because the ship was no good, or because their voyage had been misguided, but precisely because both ship and voyage had accomplished their purpose. During

the new, dry-land stage of their journey, the travelers remain—and in this illustration must never forget that they remain—the people who made *that* voyage in *that* ship.[14]

I am passionate about the Scriptures of my tradition because they have formed me into the kind of person who cares about just and compassionate treatment of others in the name of God. They have pushed me out beyond the smallness of legalism and party-spirit into a desire to see all treated justly and well. In some ways, they have even pushed me out beyond the writing on their own pages. However, I do not believe that they have pushed me past the undergirding Spirit that moves through the narratives and poetry of the text. I feel very much in line with the emphases that this Spirit is leading toward: freedom, justice and love.

Chapter Four
The Story Behind My Changing View

We usually imagine that theology is some sort of absolute and that it has been given in a more or less static way. Some things are right; some are wrong. Yet the Bible itself reflects changing opinions and understandings. A great example is that of Peter who has a vision encounter that convinces him that earlier dietary restrictions from the Old Testament are not to preclude Gentiles from receiving the Gospel (Acts 10).

Can the same thing happen today? Can God mess with our thinking if we hold too tightly to the letter of the law? Does He sometimes speak a living word into current circumstances in order to keep us from an immature understanding? I believe that He is the same yesterday, today and forever, so I opt for "yes." I've often heard people say that He can do this so long as it doesn't contradict His word (meaning the Bible), but I've given several examples already of how He does contradict His word within the Bible itself. Why should that stop?

I realize that there is a very real danger in what I'm suggesting. If nothing is solid, what is the basis for our understanding of right and wrong? Won't people feel free to do whatever they want and to create theologies that defend their decisions? I imagine that some will.

However, I'm not the first one to ponder questions like these. Paul devotes a good deal of his letter to the Galatians and also to the Romans in answering this exact dilemma. He knows that people are offended at what he has been teaching. They see him as lightening the burden of the laws and making it easier for others to sin. His answer tends to be based on his belief in the reality of the Holy Spirit. The Spirit roots and grounds our hearts in security. The Spirit leads us into new understandings. The Spirit changes our hearts and makes us long for goodness. And the Spirit empowers us on this journey of transformation. More important than a bunch of "do's and don'ts" is a new spirit within us that makes us long to love God and people, and to learn to become more like Christ ourselves.

My story of change has to do with my brother's story, with other LGBT people that I met over the years, with students who came out to me, with other students who sensed that this was the direction of God's heart long before I did, with materials that I read or watched and struggled over, and with a series of small leadings that I came to believe were from the Holy Spirit. In case it's of value to others who have struggled, I'll try to share a little of how it happened.

Rumblings

I have taught for many years at a small Christian university that specializes in a holistic form of community and travel-based education. Some time ago, one of our part-time faculty members in literature, Lorena, decided to stop teaching and go to law school. We heard from her that she was leaving her husband, who also taught for us in his field, philosophy. Before she left, she went to lunch with me and with the president of the school and explained that she had realized, against fairly strong personal resistance, that she was same-gender oriented. She had not felt safe sharing this in our community (except, I think, with a few individuals) but she had decided to do it with us for integrity's sake. We listened with respect and wished her well.

The next term, our president met Wendy Gritter, head of New Direction, a ministry that counsels and walks forward into life with LGBT people and their families. He invited her to come to speak to our student body. I remember thinking this was a mistake. Our students loved the professor who had recently left, and I felt that someone coming and addressing them about the broken nature of homosexuals would not be well received. In fact, I thought it might stir up a certain level of campus mistrust and unrest.

But Wendy amazed me. She had also been the Canadian representative of Exodus, a ministry that existed in order to help "heal" homosexuals through various forms of therapy, but she had resigned that position. She explained to our students that ministries like Exodus were promoted on miracle stories of "turn-around," often from 20 years earlier. The message of the ministry had been, "Come to us and God will change you." After years of watching deep commitment fail to result in orientation change, and realizing that this message had only added to the pain and confusion of many people, Wendy said that their new message was, "Forgive us for Message # 1; now, let's journey together knowing God will be with you and so will we." When she shared this, she won the heart of our students with her honesty and humility; it felt as though a weight had been lifted.

Some time after that, Wendy invited me to act as an outside consultant for the Board of Directors for New Direction. She had decided that this ministry needed its own new direction. She called it "generous spaciousness." I loved this concept. No longer intent on changing homosexual orientation, she had begun to see the need for helping Christian communities agree to maintain unity in spite of diverse beliefs related to this topic.

It made sense. When I looked at our own congregation, it seemed obvious that many older people felt that the way to be faithful to God was to see homosexuality as a "degrading passion" and a sinful behaviour in light of their understanding of the passages that mentioned it in the New Testament. When I turned my gaze toward our younger members, they seemed to think that the way to be faithful to God was to sense the Spirit within the words of the message, encouraging people to treat others with justice and love. When I finally got around to preaching on this topic, I spoke of "two kinds of faithfulness; one kind of love." I suggested that it was easy to respect where both groups were coming from as they both sincerely wanted to please God. That desire was the basis for our unity; the fact that we came to opposite conclusions about how to do it provided diversity. It all worked, I said, so long as we treated all people, including those with whom we disagreed, with dignity and respect.

Over these years I spoke a few times with two gay students, one in our graduate theology program, and one in our undergraduate arts program. I respected them both completely, but was unsure what to think about their orientation. I remember saying to one of them, "Whatever happens, whatever you decide to do, you are so much more to me than your sexuality. I will not stop supporting you and valuing your friendship."

But I was torn between my genuine affection for these guys and my fear that all-out support would contradict the Scriptures I had tried to base my life upon. Everything seemed confusing at this point.

Gradually, things began to change. One night there was an open panel discussion at the university to discuss approaches to different sexuality. I was asked to be one of the panel members. The professor who had left to go to law school was also going to return and speak on the panel. I knew that I had to decide what I thought. For many years I have used a prayer exercise to help me when I need clarity and focus. I simply write a letter to God, outlining my thoughts and questions. Then I wait until I hear a response rising quietly inside of me. I try to avoid "thinking" my way to an answer but wait instead for the freefall, spontaneous thought that emerges. If I write it down, there's usually more to come. I can often tap into a flow that goes for a paragraph or more. I have not thought of this as real or direct communication with God (something that I do believe is possible for humans); rather, I have seen it as a kind of "right-brain" exploration of my own deepest feelings. It wouldn't surprise me to learn that there's a level of inspiration to some of it, but I wouldn't feel comfortable claiming that. Here's what happened when I began to ask God about this issue in my journal, a couple of weeks before the panel discussion (January, 2011):

Please give wisdom about the "gay" thing. With two new people that we really love declaring themselves on this side of the equation, there is more need than ever to figure out how to articulate a position of love and yet speak with justice and wisdom for all.

I don't feel very much connection with people who automatically assume that gay people cannot please You or love You. On the other hand, there are still so few great models of mature gay Christian spirituality that I can believe in—at least I don't know too many candidates.[1]

My Son, I love everybody. I am there for everyone. I built this world and the people in it and they are all precious to Me. Some make choices that lead them away from Me and from My desires. Others are forced into bad or difficult situations. It is all too complex for you to figure out. You are, however, on safe ground if you try to honestly love and honour each person that you meet. Do not see sexual orientation; see a heart in need of Me. Do not make snap judgments (each case is different anyway); try to help each person know that I love and respect them. I treat each person in the world with dignity and respect. You are safely loving if you do the same. You are not condoning or compromising or fighting for or advocating; neither are you ignoring or denying or pretending that you have it all figured out. You don't. Neither do the people who are sure that they know what right and wrong is regarding this issue and others like it. I would like you all to trust Me beyond your thoughts about things. The world is big, and I am working in a way that you would find hard to imagine. Some of it becomes clear over time, but some of it you will not be able to see from a finite perspective. In the meantime, treat everyone with love.

Abba, I like this and feel that it does have some of Your wisdom in it, but what about other questions? Can we share in church life with gay folk, can we let them progress as though there is no "glass ceiling"? What if someone wants to lead a small group? What if someone wants to preach? What if someone wants to lead worship?

You already know the answer. None of the people that you have doing these things, including yourself, is perfect. Not one of them is entirely sexually whole. How can this be any different? You take a whole and balanced picture of people and you try to ascertain whether or not the ways in which they are tending toward wholeness are greater

> than the ways in which they are tending toward disintegration. This involves a whole life perspective; do not get hung up on the first thing you see about a person, whether or not he or she has a gay orientation or is living with someone or is wrestling with an addiction or whatever. Just look for the whole, positive, balance and trust that people are in relationship with Me and moving toward greater or lesser integration. When you sense that it is more positive than negative, you can be free to let them share their gifts with others who are also in process.

I read this to everyone at the panel and was pleased with the sense that it struck a chord in some of the audience. It resonated fairly deeply with me, too. I was starting to believe that I was finally coming to peace with what I thought.

More Light

And then one weekend Wendy came back. I can't remember the timing too well, but she was doing some meetings in our province and asked if I would like her to stop over in our town. I quickly said I would, but then I asked what kind of meeting would be most profitable—would she like to meet with a large group of people or a smaller group of leaders? She chose the second option, so we had the meeting in our living room. There was the head of a Christian denomination, a NT scholar, a couple of philosophy professors, a sociology professor, and my wife and me. I remember being surprised that most of the participants were open to considering homosexual union as a God-honouring option.

But the great thing for me that night happened after our talk. I asked Wendy if we could pray for her, as I thought she probably faced quite a bit of push-back for some of the things she was teaching in church circles. She said that she was happy to have us pray. We gathered around her. When it was my turn I prayed an image that had filled my imagination soon after we began: I saw Jesus rolling out a lengthy welcome mat in front of her. After the prayers she told us this story. Because of her role at New Direction, many gay and lesbian people had found their way to the church she attended. One day a speaker from Africa said some harsh and exclusionary things without being aware of how many people he was hurting. Everyone looked to see what Wendy would do. She thought of a welcome mat her pastor had bought for the church, declaring it to be a place of hospitality, and she went and got it. Then she rolled it out at the front and said, "If the church is not welcoming to all, it is not welcoming at all."

For me, this story began to have an importance that was in line with the vision that Peter received about eating with the Gentiles. It wouldn't leave me alone. Of course, it might have been based upon a coincidence, but what if it wasn't? What if God was using the language of prayer to confirm that He was very appreciative of people like Wendy who were going out on a limb to teach others to accept and include people of different sexuality?

Adding Fuel to the Fire

Another thing happened that year. Dan, the undergraduate student I mentioned previously, decided to speak openly to our whole community. We have a tradition at the university called Windows. Fourth-year students have the opportunity to take a chapel session and tell their life story. When Dan got ready to do his there was a buzz and I think virtually every person associated with the school came to hear what he had to say. The room was packed. When we heard about the anguish he felt as a young person, we grieved with him. But when he talked about sharing one on one with each person in his class and being accepted by all, and his gradual sense of belonging and peace, there was a palpable joy in the room.

Actually, a very similar chapel had taken place a year or two before as the graduate student I spoke of told his story. Both were so well respected, so loved; our community felt privileged to have them in our midst and honoured that they shared their stories so openly. We saw this as courage and rejoiced at the vulnerability they each displayed.

Here is something of Dan's story in his own words:

> My coming out process started years ago, and the hardest person that I had to tell was also the first: myself. I come from a family with Mennonite heritage, I went to a Dutch Reformed Christian elementary school, and attended an evangelical church every Sunday. These all gave me a pretty strict idea of what sexuality was supposed to look like. There was a pattern: boys are supposed to like girls and vice versa. Anything outside of that pattern was deemed deviant or sinful.
>
> However, when I was going through puberty, I realized that I felt no attraction to girls but that I did feel attracted to guys. Having no interest in being damned to hell, all through adolescence I prayed earnestly for change and wanted so desperately to be "normal." I didn't talk to anyone for years because I didn't know who to tell. With all the Christians that I respected, I didn't tell any

of them because I was too afraid of rejection or being treated differently afterwards. And I didn't want to tell anyone else because they might not understand the difficulty that I was having in relation between this and my faith. After going through cycles of depression, I finally decided to reach out to my high school guidance counsellor and she was a lifeline. It didn't suddenly make everything better, but reaching out and telling that first person outside of myself sure helped ease some of my fear. I still didn't like the fact that I was attracted to guys and even tried to "make" myself like girls. I thought that if I could just start a relationship with someone by going on dates, then maybe I would develop an attraction for them as it went on. I soon realized that this was a fruitless effort that would only hurt both parties.

The decision to go to St. Stephen's University, a Christian university in New Brunswick, was ultimately a great one. It was there that I could ask questions, wrestle with my faith, talk to people with a variety of views and build great friendships in a safe community. I was trying to figure out "who I was" and still went through cycles of depression. But in my later years there, as I found the confidence to talk to friends and professors about my sexuality, my fear of rejection dissipated as I came to experience love without strings attached. Instead of being pressured to think a certain way I encountered friends who encouraged and respected me.

In time, I have come to accept the fact that I am gay. To me, these are not deviant desires or anything to be ashamed of. I know that I have been "fearfully and wonderfully made." I am a beautiful child of God. I am loved. My life has a purpose. I am, in my own imperfect way, trying to follow after the life that Jesus modelled: one of loving God and loving others.

Now I know that some may not agree with what they term my "lifestyle." I can empathize; I've been there myself and know the arguments well. But I'm not seeking out an argument or debate; I'm just sharing my story.

In conclusion, I offer a quotation taken from my undergraduate thesis which focused on issues of inclusion and sexuality:

"It is not an easy process, but responding [to Otherness] by building bridges instead of putting up walls is an effort of love that is worth the chaos."

Dan's undergraduate thesis presentation was special. He chose to study three works by the British author, E. M. Forster. The first, *Howard's End* is a tale of class warfare and economic division. The next, *A Passage to India*, examines struggles related to ethnicity. The last, *Maurice*, was published posthumously and reflects Forster's own struggles with same-gender orientation. At the end of his presentation Dan spoke eloquently about the need for justice in each of these arenas, particularly the last. He pointed out that research has demonstrated that same-gender attracted young people are many times more likely to attempt suicide if they come from non-accepting families.[2] What an irony! All these families want to do is love their children and help them to have a better life. However, by not understanding that they did not choose their orientation, by treating them as sinners and outsiders, they actually harm the very ones they love the most. When will it end? Many millions of people have been deeply influenced by the adherents of conservative Christianity as they have tried to remain faithful to their understanding of the Bible. As Dan said, what if only 2% of the children of these families grow up attracted to their own genders (he was intentionally presenting a lower number than studies suggest). That represents a lot of people in pain. Think of the mental and emotional torture that this causes, and then compound it with the belief of many that they are deserving of hell as they leave this life. When all that is ahead, both in this life and the next, looks like a constant experience of rejection, is it any wonder that so many have given up?

Dan's presentation was met with a spontaneous standing ovation. Those in attendance appreciated the courage to say such things. Later, when he was given a full-tuition scholarship to one of Canada's top law schools, we could not have been more prouder.

The Lens You Choose ...

I think this issue took a sabbatical in my experience over the next year. When it did come up in conversation, I realized that I had already moved quite a distance from the perspective of my early life. One day someone wrote to our university to ask about our stand on various human rights issues. As our management committee talked about how to answer this simple question, an idea popped into my head and out my mouth: *"we don't have a position; we have people."* Over time I've come to think that this is actually a fairly profound statement. Why on earth should all the people in an institution be expected to believe the same things or think the same way? Perhaps some would think that a situation like this would reflect spiritual faithfulness, but it is actually the antithesis of true spirituality. What it indicates is a kind of cookie-cutter pattern that has been foisted upon group members. Probably no one has pointed out the dangers of such a posture better than Jean Vanier, Canadian founder of L' Arche, an international organization that cares for handicapped people through the building of caring communities. In *Community and Growth* he writes,

> Too many communities form—or deform—their members to make them all alike, as if this were a good quality, based on self-denial. These communities are founded on laws or rules. But it is the opposite which is important; each person must grow in their gift to build the community and make it more beautiful and more radiant, a clearer sign of the Kingdom.[3]

Remember that Paul said, "Where the Spirit of the Lord is, there is liberty" (2 Cor. 3:17). Presumably this includes the freedom to think. It also includes the freedom to emphasize different priorities in the interpretation of Scripture. It allows us to interpret toward love.

What Happened Next

All of this relates to the bomb that went off in our community. During Dan's time at the university there was at least one other undergraduate gay student, though none of us knew it at the time. What we did know was that Ashley was severely troubled, in extreme emotional distress. And yes, there was talk of suicide; it was a very real danger. After finishing at school she worked for awhile but left a job over stress-related issues. In the months that followed, unemployed, it seemed that she got lower and lower. I spoke with her several times and wondered what could help her. Finally something did. It involved many levels, I'm sure, but it included an encouragement through counselling to accept that it was better to be a healthy same-gender oriented person than to be a tormented person with an undisclosed problem. Gradually life came into balance for Ashley. She got a new job, doing something she loved, and she met the love of her life, Kathryn. They travelled from Ontario to New Brunswick the next year to attend our convocation. Together they were lovely, and Ashley was at peace. It felt so much better to see her this way. At a breakfast at our home, she told me that Wendy Gritter had been a help to her, too. And she shared something she had heard Wendy teach.

Christian churches tend to characterize same-gender orientation under four headings, and each of these can be seen to have an appropriate and corresponding response. Some think of it as rebellion, so the response is thought to be repentance. Some think of it as addiction, calling for a response of abstinence. Some think of it as brokenness (in the sense that not everything works out perfectly in a broken world), so the need is for grace. And some think of it as variant or different, calling for the appropriate response of celebration.

Ashley looked at me over breakfast and said this: "I don't really relate to the first two (rebellion or addiction). And I don't know whether my situation is brokenness or variant, but I find that I can live with either of these." I was blown away by her wisdom and her humility. I also felt that she reflected an inner wholeness and balance that I had longed to see in her for quite some time.

It was a year later that Ashley and Kathryn married. Their celebration was in Ontario, and it was the same weekend that our son, Noah, married Cara, another of our graduates, not too far away. We weren't able to go to Ashley and Kathryn's wedding as we prepared for our family celebration, but others from our community went and we heard that it was lovely. We were happy for them. Our own celebration seemed outstanding to us. Cara's family was generous and welcoming and we felt as though we had been grafted into a new and rich part of life. The day after the wedding I had to fly to England to teach in a theological program there. I was gone for a week. When Mary Ellen picked me up at the airport the next Saturday night, it was already Sunday morning! We got home an hour or so later, in the middle of the night, and I was happy that I had asked someone else to bring the talk at church that day. We went, though, and I asked Mary Ellen to put together a small slide show of wedding pictures as many people knew Noah and Cara.

When I entered the hall of the old school that our church purchased some years ago, there were many dear friends to meet after a couple of weeks away. And suddenly I realized that Ashley and Kathryn were there, too. They had honeymooned in Nova Scotia and had decided to drive almost six hours from Halifax that morning in order to come to church. I was thrilled to see them but it occurred to me that I couldn't show our pictures and share our joy without making reference to theirs. Our church tends to be very welcoming and loving. We have worked hard at not being judgmental toward anyone. Most of our folks are very honest about difficulties that they have faced in life. In fact, I sometimes refer to our church as the "island of broken toys," a phrase I remembered from an old TV Christmas special. The implication is that we all have "stuff" and there's no need to give anyone else a hard time! We also have a lesbian couple that visit us some summers to see their children and grandchildren and, as far as I know, they have always been well received. But I suspected that the affirmation of a lesbian wedding would be a stretch for some people. I just didn't know how much. I felt pretty sure that if I prefaced my comments about Ashley and Kathryn with some sort of qualification, everyone would be ok. As soon as I thought of that, though, I rejected the idea. To qualify their love would be to diminish it, and I refused to do that.

So I showed the pictures of Noah and Cara and expressed our family's delight in the whole experience. Then I asked another couple to stand that had been married two weeks before. Everyone cheered (we're a pretty informal group). Then I asked Ashley and Kathryn to stand to be congratulated as well. People cheered and applauded once more. I later heard that there were also a few gasps ....

Over the next couple of weeks I began to realize that a whole slice of our congregation had disappeared. And I heard that some people who were staying were upset, but I didn't know who they were. It didn't really trouble me because I thought I had done the right thing. Welcoming people without judgment (our typical stance) had been okay, I guess, but publicly celebrating a marriage seemed to some like an inappropriate political statement. I actually hadn't meant it that way—I was just trying to welcome and honour the people involved. I wasn't trying to say that I was for or against gay marriages. I hadn't even thought all of that through. I did know that I was for Ashley and Kathryn, though. And I was pretty sure God was as well.

It all got a little worse for me when I learned that some of our dearest colleagues were among the most upset. I hated the idea of hurting people, especially people that I loved and have shared so much of life with. Gradually an inner frenzy began to take away my own sense of peace.

Two weekends after the incident, I found that I couldn't get quiet enough on the inside in order to prepare a sermon for Sunday morning. On Saturday there was a country fair at our local nature park and I encouraged Mary Ellen and a friend who was staying with us to go without me. I was wrestling deeply and quite troubled. I sat alone through part of the morning in our living room with a Bible, but I didn't open it for a long time. I don't think I prayed coherently, either. I just sat and asked God to help me to figure it all out. What was right? Had I done the wrong thing? I knew that I had hurt people that I loved and respected, but I couldn't imagine playing it out in a different way.

Finally, I opened the Bible. I asked God where to read and I felt a kind of inner direction toward the New Testament letter of 1 John. It was a strange choice because it has nothing directly to do with the topic, but I have loved this letter over the years. Maybe it was simply familiarity that drew me to it. As I read I did see a few things in a new light, and I was glad that I was there. I would have had a hard time articulating what I felt, but it seemed as though there were principles just below the surface of the message that were strangely relevant. After a while, I stopped thinking about it all and went to do some other things.

When Mary Ellen and our friend returned we had dinner and planned to watch something on TV. I still felt miles away from being able to put together a talk for the morning. Then Mary Ellen did the most astonishing thing: she suggested that we listen to a recorded sermon together. Anyone who knows Mary Ellen well can see that she is the kind of person who sincerely loves God and people (I don't know of anyone who does it better), but there is not a religious bone in her body. She is not drawn to religious materials of any kind! In more than 30 years she had never suggested anything close to this. But she had a reason. I have a respect for the thinking of a certain pastor from the Boston area. His name is Dave Schmelzer. I haven't met him but I've read a couple of things by him and been impressed. Mary Ellen said that she had googled him and he had an hour talk on his website on homosexuality and church.[4] She could see that I was still troubled and she thought his perspective might be helpful.

The three of us sat in our living room and listened as Schmelzer spoke about the tendency of churches to be on one side or the other of an issue. He presented the story of the heavenly warrior in Joshua 5 as an example of a better way to see things. Joshua, troubled before a battle, sees the warrior and asks, "Are you for us or for our adversaries?" The answer is this: "No; rather I indeed come now as captain of the host of the Lord." Then, in response to a direction from this strange being, Joshua bows down and takes his shoes off. Schmelzer says that this is also the posture of Jesus in situation after situation where people come to Him for moral judgments. He doesn't normally stand on one side or another; rather, He stands for God and the people involved, somewhere far above the dichotomy of the dilemma.

Then Schmelzer turned his attention to 1 John, the focus of most of the rest of his talk. He said that there were principles there that could help us understand how to live with others in church First, he suggested that we be hard on our own troubles and learn how to bring them into the light of disclosure. Then he said we should be generous in dealing with others. If they are teaching that Jesus hasn't come in the flesh (a big deal at the time of writing), we should be very protective, but if there is anything else where we think they are doing something wrong, we should pray for them (not judge or admonish!). This sounded a lot like Jesus's teaching about the mistake of trying to remove a splinter from a neighbour's eye while we have a log in our own. And it brought a level of healing to my soul. What a coincidence that Schmelzer had been drawn to the same letter that I had and that I heard his teaching on the very same day. He ended the talk by making reference to LGBT groups that were meeting as part of their church. I felt, once again, that God was leading me and I had no trouble preparing a talk after that. It wasn't on this subject but it felt like something that was healthy and good for the community at the time. The important thing, from my perspective, was more encouragement to push toward a humble and loving inclusion of anyone that wanted to come and worship with us.

However, the issues didn't go away. People were confused. Some were upset. We decided that we would have a public forum to talk about what had happened. I wasn't sure how to lead it, but I remembered that Wendy had left a six-session video course with me the year before. It was called *Bridging the Gap: Conversations on Befriending our Gay Neighbours*. Prepared by New Direction, it presented diversity among gay Christian voices on several topics and it included counsel from a number of Christian leaders, including Tony Campolo, Brian McLaren, Bruxy Cavey, Greg Paul, and Wendy herself. I selected a couple of portions for viewing.

My senior associate at church, Walter, is also a professor at our university. His field is psychology and he is a marriage and family counsellor. Together we planned and led the evening. It was clear that there were different opinions about the way forward among the people who came to the forum. Some thought we were headed in the right direction by trying to create a place where people didn't have to agree; others wanted their church to teach the thing that they believed was right. This meant, I think, in most cases, that people wanted us to teach that homosexuals should be loved but also to be clearly instructed that we thought what they were doing was wrong. And they wanted their kids to hear that message, too. Some liked the idea of saying, "hate the sin but love the sinner." Walter, familiar with the work of Richard Beck, knew that this was actually impossible. He later explained that disgust is an obstacle to love.

Beck, in his book, *Unclean: Meditations on Purity, Hospitality, and Morality*, writes that humans learn disgust from culture, probably to safeguard them in various ways. Having a sense of disgust is universal; objects of disgust are not. Once formed, disgust gives a strong emotional basis toward interpretation and must be named before honest evaluation is possible. Beck uses the analogy of a sweet tooth to illustrate what this means. We learn to inhibit the draw of sweetness in diet so that we can live a healthy life, but it rarely loses its attractiveness for those who like it. He says,

> Striving after good theology is similar to managing a sweet tooth. Psychological dynamics will always make certain theological systems more or less appealing. And yet psychologically appealing and intuitive theological systems are not always healthy. In short, these psychological dynamics function as a sweet tooth, a kind of cognitive temptation that pulls the intellectually lazy or unreflective (because we are busy folk with day jobs) into theological orbits that hamper the mission of the church. As with managing the sweet tooth, vigilance and care are needed to keep us on a healthy path.[5]

Later in his important study Beck describes the way that love and revulsion work as opposing forces, making it impossible in reality to "hate the sin but love the sinner":

> Unless sociomoral disgust is addressed in the heart, efforts toward justice, hospitality, or charity will be, in the end, ineffective and distancing. The "will to embrace" must precede any judgments of the other. Embrace must be *deep* and should not be reduced to social or political rearrangements and accommodations.[6]

So we were at an impasse. As I said, many people felt that we were on the right track; others were worried and wondered if they could continue to be a part of our community. Everything they had ever known had taught them that God stood against homosexuality. How could they continue to be part of a church if the leaders were willing to go against the Bible? And yet, many of us had worshipped together for more than 20 years. We had worried about our kids together. We had travelled together, worked together, tried to care for people in our town together—how could any of us pull back from that?

The Way Forward

One practical suggestion came from the public forum: let's watch the rest of the video series. Several people had asked if there was any way for them to watch the entirety of *Bridging the Gap*. We decided to do an eight-week video study in our home. It was during this period that I began to realize that the Bible's teaching was far less clear than most of us had supposed. The videos were excellent, and they provided stimulating questions for group discussion. Not everyone came to a resolution regarding what he or she believed during this study, but it was healthy for us to be facing the issues together.

The Story Behind My Changing View

Some time before the first session I happened to notice that a half-hour television show called Sex + Religion was about to air on a cable network called eqhd. The promotional message said that Tony Campolo and his wife, Peggy, would be interviewed. I have always thought highly of Dr. Campolo, a sociologist from Eastern University in Pennsylvania, and I had read a brief but intriguing essay by Peggy in a book that was edited by Walter Wink.[7] Tony was featured in the *Bridging the Gap* series, so I thought some extra comments by him would be very pertinent. I decided to record and save the show.

In the end, I don't think I can overstate the importance of this show in terms of helping me come to my own sense of right and wrong regarding homosexual union. I watched it a couple of times and then decided to keep it and show it to our group at the conclusion of our study.

People from different religions shared their views, but Tony and Peggy are the main feature. I hadn't realized this, but they have opposing views on the best way forward for gay Christians. In order to bring the issues into the open, and to demonstrate that people that love each other can disagree, they have been carrying on a public debate on various university campuses. What courage! Peggy believes that homosexuals ought to build loving and faithful unions with a life-partner; Tony believes that they ought to remain celibate. She thinks that Romans 1 is about Roman orgies and has nothing to say about faithful love; he thinks that it's a declaration that homosexuality is wrong. He insists that church fathers have always seen it this way. She says that if they have, they're simply mistaken. The part that touched me the most was at the very end. Tony says this:

> Very often gay young men and young women come into this office seeking help. I advise them to be celibate. In the overwhelming number of cases the reaction to that is "it won't work for me. I've tried. I've prayed, I've gone to Pentecostal churches; I've done everything. I've gone to counseling—nothing's worked." At that point, I usually say, "Look, don't give up on God; talk to my wife. I can't in clear conscience advise you to do what she will advise you to do. But I think she can help you because what she has to say is much better than giving up on God, giving up on the church, and walking away from the love that my wife and I have for you."[8]

And Peggy interjects, "from giving up on trying to live a moral life." I think I had watched this at least three times before it hit me that they were a unit. They present different points of view, but they both do so in an empathic manner. And, when push comes to shove, Tony acknowledges that Peggy's answer is more helpful for many. He has given the standard that he believes in, but he recognizes that not everyone can pull it off. So, in the final analysis, he would rather that someone choose a faithful same-sex relationship than that he or she leave God and church behind.

This had the force of a revelation for me. I put it together with the thing I had heard Lewis Smedes say, "People have to do the best they can with what they have been given." Suddenly, this made so much sense. There are people in the world who are same-gender attracted. Perhaps there are various causes that can bring this about, but in many cases people awakened to this realization with horror. They did nothing to choose it and some would have done anything to change it. As Justin Lee points out, the simplistic answer of a distant father and an over-bearing mother is neither true nor helpful.[9] And neither are the various reparative therapies that have been foisted upon people. Some have changed their behaviour; very few, if any, have changed their orientation. And, as noted earlier, many famous examples of gay people who were "healed" by these therapies reverted over time.[10]

So what does love have to say to people who find themselves in the difficult position of being attracted to their own gender? Harsh words, rejection and trying to force change, all seem considerably less than what love would do. And yet, these have often been the prevalent responses from Christian churches—it's time for something better.

Here are some more thoughts by Lewis Smedes, who taught theology and ethics at Fuller Seminary in Pasadena for 28 years:

- I think that gays and lesbians, like the rest of us, are called to achieve the best moral relationships of love that are possible for them within the limits of a condition they did not choose.
- I think that gays and lesbians merit the same rights and bear the same responsibilities within society that anyone else does.
- I think that, if celibacy is not possible, it is better for gays and lesbians to live together in committed monogamous relationships of love than not. Same-sex partnerships that are committed offer the best moral option available.

Then he concludes,

> These are some things I have come to believe after studying the Holy Scripture, after reflecting on Christian tradition, and after trying to enrich my knowledge and discernment with the insight of love. I may be wrong. I may not be seeing reality as clearly as I think I am. I am willing to learn from those who are willing to share their discernment with me. But this is what I believe.[11]

Dr. Smedes died in 2002. In this essay, like Tony Campolo, he seems to favour celibacy but allows for union as the best moral option "if celibacy is not possible." I don't see it this way. I think that celibacy is an honourable choice and vocation for some heterosexuals as well as for some homosexuals. I don't see it as a better option than marriage for either. Hidden within the thought of both of these giants is the sense that there is something wrong with people who are same-gender attracted. They have both come a long way (not as far as Peggy!) in encouraging the Church toward a more just and honouring position, but it's not okay to divide people into classes of greater or lesser quality. It is healthier, in my opinion, to come to peace with the fact that some people are different. They need to learn what morality and faith and community mean for themselves, given the difference they experience. Others should not try to prescribe this for them.

Marriage? Why Not Civil Unions?

When Smedes spoke of "committed monogamous relationships of love," he did not define what these should be like. Over the past decade there has been a great deal of debate about this. For heterosexual Christians who want to treat LGBT people with justice and dignity, an important question comes quickly to the surface: isn't there some way to protect the rights of minority sexuality people without threatening the traditional notion of marriage as being between a man and a woman? Some believe that a form of civil union could be determined in such a way that both of these goals would be accomplished. Well-meaning people reach different conclusions. Here's what I feel:

If there is any possibility for minorities to be oppressed, the likelihood is that it will happen. Think of this as a tragic variation on Murphy's Law. Therefore, minorities must be protected to the full extent of law. If not, vulnerabilities are sure to be exposed at some point.

The person who helped me to realize this is David Anderson, pastor of Bridgeway Community Church in Baltimore, Maryland, one of America's preeminent multicultural congregations. He wrote a book called *Gracism: the Art of Inclusion*. From it I learned that it's not enough to treat people in a neutral manner after centuries or decades of oppression; rather, in place of racism there must come *gracism*. This is a determination to lift and protect those who have been under the burden of social prejudice. Anderson says,

> I define racism as speaking, acting or thinking negatively about someone else solely based on that person's color, class or culture. A common definition for grace is the unmerited favor of God on humankind. Extending such favor and kindness upon other human beings is how we Christians demonstrate this grace practically from day to day. When one merges the definition of racism, which is negative, with grace, which is positive, a new term emerges—*gracism*. I define gracism as the positive extension of favor on other humans based on color, class or culture.[12]

I endorse gay marriage because I believe that it is the only safe way to lift and protect the rights of people with different sexuality. I understand and appreciate the thinking of many that an alternative arrangement such as civil unions would be fair, but I don't believe that anything less than marriage will give full protection. There should not be any possibility for legal manipulations that will allow prejudiced people to marginalize and hurt others. For Christians who feel stretched by this idea, think of it like this: we are to walk the second mile. This is an allusion to something that Jesus taught in the Sermon on the Mount. "Whoever forces you to go one mile, go with him two" (Matt. 5:41). This teaching is followed by another: "Give to him who asks of you, and do not turn away from him who wants to borrow from you" (Matt. 5:42). And then there is the exhortation to love enemies (verse 44). The spirit of these verses is clear: we are not to promote our own agenda; rather, we are meant to care for the needs of others. This is how we are to demonstrate the heart of the Father, in a spirit of gracism.

Sarah's Story

As this year progressed and my own position solidified, I came into contact with another of our former students who had discovered that she was gay. Unfortunately, this realization came after she had married a young man she had met at our university. The marriage didn't last and, of course, it was a difficult time for both of them. After some correspondence I asked if she would be willing to share some of her story with me. She gladly did, and I found it so moving that I asked if I could share it with others. In her letter to me she makes mention of "someone prophesying over me at the Vineyard." This was a church that she attended while she was growing up.

> I dropped out of college for many years after the divorce, because I needed to make a living.

Everyone was in a lot of pain during those years, and we all isolated ourselves from one another. It was particularly hard with my parents and church folks. They saw me as an embarrassment and abomination to God. I internalized that and withdrew and went into a deep depression. I thought I was stupid, unlovable, and unworthy. I tried partying, drinking, and dating away the sadness but nothing worked. I wasn't healthy at that time and I wasn't capable of having healthy relationships. I used to cry myself to sleep and wish I would not wake up (don't worry there is a happy ending). I thought God hated me as much as I thought my family did during those years ... and that was the worst heartache I have ever experienced.

At first, I rejected God. Then, I tried studying other religions I could find. I was hoping to find another "god" who would accept me. The closest I came was Buddhism, but it still didn't feed my soul like my relationship with Christ. So, I basically decided that I was going to pretend God didn't exist and reject all religion once again. I call these my humanist years.

Eventually I ended up getting a sweet job working as a manager at a bank. They had tuition reimbursement and I decided to go back to school. I needed to get out of Maine, because it was a really sad and depressing place for me. At 26, I took a leap of faith and transferred my job to North Carolina where I attended a Quaker school called Guilford College. I didn't know it was Quaker. I was supposed to go somewhere else in the same town but when I drove by Guilford the week before school started something in my spirit told me to apply there. I did, and I was accepted almost immediately.

Guilford had a degree program called "Justice and Policy Studies." Essentially it was a combination of sociology, criminal justice, and peace studies. I LOVED the program and took 16-20 credit hours every semester in the evenings while working full time at the bank. I worked and studied non-stop but the program and the professors I met changed my life. I graduated from Guilford in 2009 with the highest GPA in the class and winning the departmental award of excellence. At the ceremony, the head of the department gave a small speech and said that she always loved my "intellectual courage" and that everyone in our program who met me adored me—not bad for someone who thought she was stupid and unlovable just years before. I went to my professors often during that time and one of them mentioned a church she thought I should try.

I visited the church which was in Charlotte (where I live now) and fell in love. The church is predominately African-American and rooted in Black Spiritual traditions. However, they are an affirming church and have many members who are LGBT and allowed to serve in ministry. I joined the dance ministry and eventually led the team at the church. The first time I walked in I looked around and saw tons of gay people and even transgender people serving in ministry. I started crying immediately. I didn't understand how God could love people "like us"—I cried every time I walked in for the first two years. Every single time. From the moment of the first prayer until the benediction I cried. I sat through sermons with tears streaming down my face. I had years and years of pain and self-hatred that just started busting out of me. I started feeling the love of God again, healing the deepest parts of me. I could go on forever about this part of my life. Instead, I'll just say that being a part of the church and attending therapy for a few years really helped me get healthy and happy again. I haven't been depressed or in despair since the day I realized that I really am a beautiful creation of God—without condition, without having to earn it, without having to make myself different. Just as I am. Totally and completely loved.

I applied to law school and knew I was supposed to stay in Charlotte. I got in, did the law school thing, worked in DC during the summer, had great jobs during law school, and now I'm about to graduate. I remember someone prophesying over me at the Vineyard saying that God had called me to help the most marginalized in our community, even when people don't understand. The prophecy explained that people were going to reject me because of the work I will do but that I am never to forget that it is the call of God. True to that prophecy, I have found my calling. I am opening an LGBT Legal Center here in Charlotte to help eliminate barriers to justice for LGBT people. Our center's programs will focus on helping LGBT people of color and specifically transgender individuals. Professionally, I'll be a lawyer. Spiritually, I'll be helping the people no one cares about (transgender people, sex workers, low-income people of color, and lesbian and gay people) create and build a life that they will love living. Other Christians may judge this work, but I know it is the Lord's. I'll never forget the loneliness I felt during my first years coming out, and that memory has created space for immense compassion and love that I never imagined. It is that love and compassion that propels me to this day.

And I am very grateful for my journey.

I am more moved than I can say by Sarah's letter. She has put into words something that I feel is very close to the heart of God. Personally, I believe the prophetic calling to the "last and the least" was very much from a God who loves the people that everyone else tends to reject. How is this not like the message of the parable in Matthew 25: 31-46? What we do to "the least of these" we do to Christ Himself.

Chapter Five
Can We Really Have New Thoughts?

Our Scriptures encourage faithful clinging to tradition. Listen, for instance, to these words from the Book of Jeremiah:

> Thus says the Lord, "Stand by the ways and see and ask for the ancient paths, where the good way is, and walk in it; and you will find rest for your souls ..." (Jer. 6:16).

But there are indications that the old needs to give way to the new. Somehow the two need to blend and meet together. Here is a passage that suggests this is possible:

> 7 Beloved, I am not writing a new commandment to you, but an old commandment which you have had from the beginning; the old commandment is the word which you have heard. 8 On the other hand, I am writing a new commandment to you, which is true in Him and in you, because the darkness is passing away and the true Light is already shining (1 John 2:7,8).

The new grows out of the old and shares the same character, but it need not be limited by what has gone before. Probably the most interesting passage of Scripture that deals with this thought is found in the Letter to the Galatians:

> There is neither Jew nor Greek, there is neither slave nor free man, there is neither male nor female; for you are all one in Christ Jesus (Gal. 3:28).

It was years ago, in a graduate class in marriage and family counselling, that a professor encouraged us to ask questions of this text. When did the Christian Church focus on the need to bridge the distinction between Jew and Gentile? When did slavery become an important ethical issue for the Church? When did the distinction between men and women become a focus of justice? The answers are provocative. The need for Jew and Gentile to come together is the focus of a good part of the New Testament—it was a first century issue. But slavery didn't grab the ethical attention of the Church in a widespread fashion until the late 18th and early 19th centuries. That one took some time. What follows is obvious—in many places women are not yet treated with equality in the Christian world. When will that take place? According to this passage, there ought not to be any ethnic, economic or gender distinctions in the followers of Christ, but that has not been the story through a good deal of church history.

I have come to believe that the Holy Spirit gives new paradigms of consciousness as we grow. We need new wine skins as well as new wine. It can take us a very long time to understand things, but the Spirit is moving all of us toward a just and compassionate care for others. Many people look at history and see moral decay. I see the opposite. I believe that the Kingdom of God is advancing. I sometimes think that it is doing this in spite of the best efforts of the Christian Church. Jesus felt especially connected to Isaiah's description of a suffering servant. In fact, Matthew tells us that He intentionally followed this model in His own life and ministry (Matt 12; see Is. 42:1-4). This passage that meant so much to Him indicates that the result of the Servant's work will be a never-ending increase of justice. I believe we are seeing that.

Just for fun, I've been calling it *The-volution*, with the first part of this word coming from the Greek *Theos*, or God. I believe that God has been leading our understanding toward justice and goodness, but it can be a fairly hard sell. We can be very slow to follow.

What evidence is there that things are getting better? Perhaps not too much if someone has his or her mind focused on a nostalgically romantic period of goodness and faithfulness that never actually existed. Greg Boyd brilliantly points this out in *The Myth of a Christian Nation*. He questions the pretense of his own country at moral nationhood by bringing up the uncomfortable realities of lands stolen from indigenous peoples and wealth produced on the backs of slaves.[1] But there is some clear evidence of growing goodness in the way we have begun to believe that women and minorities must be protected and treated with equality.

I receive a devotional message each morning from Inward/Outward, a service of The Church of the Saviour in Washington, DC. Not long ago there was a quote from a 19th century Unitarian minister named Theodore Parker. Parts of this quote can be found in the sermons of Martin Luther King, Jr.[2] It reads:

> Look at the facts of the world. You see a continual and progressive triumph of the right. I do not pretend to understand the moral universe, the arc is a long one, my eye reaches but little ways. I cannot calculate the curve and complete the figure by the experience of sight; I can divine it by conscience. But from what I see I am sure it bends toward justice.[3]

This is my feeling, too. We are on the move toward greater understanding, and the clearest evidence of this is how the last and the least are treated in our societies. It probably doesn't need to be clarified, but Parker's assertion that there is "a triumph of the right" is not about political loyalties. He means a triumph of goodness and a direction toward justice.

Gwynne Dyer, an independent journalist and military historian, recently said this:

> We live in an era where, for the first time in history, no great power genuinely fears attack by any other, and where the number of actual wars can be counted on the fingers of one badly mutilated hand.
>
> Almost 90 million people died in the world wars and other big wars (including the Russian, Chinese, and Spanish civil wars) of the first half of the 20th century, out of a world population that was one-third of what it is now. In the second half of the century the death toll dropped steeply to 25 million or so, most of whom died in colonial independence wars and civil wars.
>
> And so far, in the 21st century, the total is less than one million people killed in war. What we have on our hands here is a miraculous and mostly unsung success story. There will doubtless be more wars, but they may be small and infrequent. We are obviously doing something right.

We should figure out what it is, and do more of it.[4]

I find a correspondence between Dyer's view and that of Hans Rosling, the Swedish medical doctor, statistician, and professor of global health. Rosling has presented a startling four-minute BBC Four video that gives an examination of average health and wealth for 200 countries over the past 200 years.[5] He demonstrates by charting over 120,000 numbers that virtually all countries had low life expectancy and low average income in 1810. But almost all are significantly advanced from that point now. Something is working.

Add to this voting privileges being extended to minorities, revulsion at segregated societies, a sense of responsibility for colonial blunders, and the growing consciousness of the status of women; it is clear that some good things are happening. And yet, there is obviously a long way to go.

I think there is another arena in life where it is also possible to see some marked advances: theology. Not all the world is aware, and neither is a good deal of the church, but there have been many refreshing ideas in the past century or so. We are moving toward a more humane form of religion. Some may see this as deplorable; I think we are on the right track.

Here are some of the changes that I've noticed. I call it a Starter's List of Evolving Christian Ideas:

a) God is not the emotionless abstraction of Greek philosophy that deeply influenced a great deal of Christian theology.

b) In fact, as Isaiah 63 affirms, God suffers along with people in their afflictions.

c) The ancient Greek dichotomy between spirit and matter is unhelpful.

d) Sexuality, therefore, as expressed within proper boundaries is a great good, not a compromise with a flawed material universe.

e) Also, the whole created order is important and we are meant to be good stewards of it.

f) We are witnessing improved attitudes toward different races and toward women.

g) There is a general recognition that various cultures (and religions) have different worldviews and strengths that it would be appropriate to learn from.

h) We no longer see culture as evil in and of itself (most of us would now repent for trying to bring culture along with the Gospel to other nations as though our culture and even language—think of the residential schools—provided the only or the best access to Jesus).

i) There is a belief that the different Christian denominations have strengths that we can learn from and that they can work together.

j) A "more hopeful anthropology" (over and against "worm theology") is beginning to grow— we are the image/idols of the Creator on earth and goodness, however flawed, is at our core.

k) There is a healthier sense of how to please God (we are beginning to abandon asceticism in favour of trust).

l) There is a growing belief that we should take the Golden Rule seriously, especially as it relates to enemies or people that are different than we are.

m) God is being seen less as an abstract Judge and more as a Loving Participant who chooses to flow through life in a helpful way with people.[6]

n) There is a growing belief that we live in the tension of the "already, but not yet," of the Kingdom of God, and that we can play a meaningful role in doing God's work in the world, in line with the way that Jesus and His disciples did it (in other words, our faith is based on action and participation with God rather than on knowledge alone).

Many of these represent attitudinal shifts that are less than 100 years old. Like it or not, we are in motion. I believe we are experiencing *The-volution*! I do not think we should be afraid of more change; rather, particularly if it can be seen to be in line with the character of Jesus, we should embrace it and walk with freedom into a more just and compassionate future.

Chapter Six
What is the Importance of the Bible?

In spite of what I've written about misusing the Bible as a rulebook, I believe that it is an invaluable aid to Christian growth and maturity. I see it as a training ground, a trysting place, a source of wisdom, a traffic light, a directional sign and an icon. Some of these blend together in my understanding but I'll try to clarify what I mean.

As a training ground, the Bible shows the things that God loves and the things that repel Him. Caring for those who are weak and broken is high on the list in both testaments. Doing this with kindness and mercy instead of arrogance and judgment are also important. Working humbly with Him in order to develop our own lives allows Him to enrich our experience immeasurably. And reaching out to care, in whatever ways we are good at, fills life with meaning and with joy.

In the midst of the training, the Bible is actually a trysting place—it can be the place between the visible and invisible world where authentic transactions of the soul are encouraged. St. Augustine said,

> For I know of no other book so destructive of pride, so potent a weapon to crush your enemies and all who are on their guard against you, refusing to be reconciled with you and trying to justify the wrong that they do. O Lord, I know no written words so pure as these, none that have induced me so firmly to make my confession to you, none that have so eased for me the task of bowing my neck to your yoke or so gently persuaded me to worship you for your sake and not for mine. Let me understand them, good Father. Grant me this gift, for I submit myself to them, and it was for those who submit themselves that you made this solid shield.[1]

I know what he means, even if I wouldn't have said it in exactly the same way. I struggle with the "crush your enemies" part. But I have had countless experiences of reading the Bible and suddenly knowing that I have been treating others badly by insisting on my own way. I get lost in a story and the next thing I know, a conflict with someone at home or at work plays out before my mind and I realize that I acted or spoke selfishly. Then my heart softens and I often, not always, find a way to build a bridge to the other person.

The Bible is full of many forms of literature and it is, I'm sure, fully human at the same time as it is imbued with divine inspiration, but I think everyone would have to admit that it's a source of wisdom. Even if someone rejected belief in a personal God, there's a lot in it about how to get along with people, or how to grow and mature through difficulties. St. Paul's encouragement to rejoice in all things and focus on the positive seems strangely contemporary in light of happiness studies done by Shawn Achor from Harvard. These demonstrate that people who train their brains to see the good do better at many aspects of life.[2] Countless studies, none more important than Desmond Tutu's *No Future Without Forgiveness*,[3] demonstrate the psychological and political relevance of the Bible's message about this topic.

But I see the Bible as a source of immediate wisdom, too. This is a little difficult to explain but I'll give it a shot.

When I was first introduced to Biblical Studies it seemed common for people to teach that there were two major ways to study the Bible, devotionally and academically. Devotional reading was the daily exercise of coming to the Scriptures in search of a meeting with God. Believers were encouraged to read a small portion, perhaps one verse, perhaps a chapter or two, and to savour the implications of the words. Usually they were advised to relate them to their own lives and situations. Sometimes they were encouraged to find the Word within the words; that is, to look for the message that God was speaking to them personally through the verses that they read.

Academic reading was somewhat different. It generally focused on larger portions and systematic study until whole parts of the Bible were devoured and hopefully understood. The academic approach emphasized knowledge of historical background. It asked questions of the text. When was this portion written? What was the context? Who wrote it? Why? To whom was it addressed? What was the overall point? How was the message conveyed? Students were encouraged to learn Greek and Hebrew so that they could see if there were any subtleties in the text that weren't easily or accurately communicated by English translations.

Both of these approaches are valid. Devotional reading helps us to develop intimacy in our relationship with God; academic work allows us to have a better understanding of the message that He has given to the world through the Scriptures—it helps us to have a better sense of what He loves and what He hates. Both approaches together can lead beyond mere knowledge to the acquisition of wisdom.

However, as I have worked over the years as a pastor as well as a teacher, I've come to believe that there is another important approach to the Bible. I'm not sure I believed in this Third Way for a large part of my Christian life. Now I am often delighted by it. I think it involves the wedding of the other two approaches with the gift of prophecy. As we do our best to build a relationship with God through a devotional life and serious study, and add to this a growing sense of trust and obedience, we build a deeper level of intimacy with Him. This makes it possible for Him to communicate with us more often on a direct or immediate level. He speaks to us. Often what he has to say comes in the wrapping of a Scriptural phrase or story.

With the precision of a super-computer, or that of the most expert surgeon, the Holy Spirit seems to love to direct believers to the one passage in the Bible best-suited to "tell their story." I've seen it again and again. Now I sometimes think of the Bible as a wonderful collection of thousands of "life bubbles." Only God really knows what is going on in someone's life, but as people come around that person to pray, a certain Scripture passage becomes the focus of the prayer. The next day it may appear in a devotional book that the person has been reading. Two days later an old friend might call and share it again. It may very well be the focus of the next sermon that is heard. And as the person learns to interpret reality through the construction of the biblical passage, life is reborn in them, and they grow.

There have been times that paying attention to subtle messages like these helped me to make decisions that affected my life and work in powerful and positive ways. I'm for it.

The traffic light idea is in line with this. I may have determined that it's important to talk with someone or to present an idea at work. A little time in the Bible, not thinking directly about whatever issue is on my mind, seems to give either encouragement to go for it, caution about how to do it, or a sense of "wait!" This tends to connect the trysting place and the source of wisdom ideas. Simply being there, with as open a heart as possible, seems to allow a quiet interior sense that relates to timing. I don't try to make this happen; but I notice that it sometimes does.

As a directional sign, the Bible points to Jesus. It does this in remarkable ways. I am convinced that there is a level of literary foreshadowing that demonstrates a Super-intelligence behind the writings in the book. Perhaps I will write more about this someday. In the meantime, let me just point out that there are only stories in the Book of Genesis about five of Jacob's 12 sons. Joseph's story is told because it, ultimately, explains how all the tribes became slaves in Egypt. Other than that, there are stories of the four oldest sons. Three are problem stories, explaining why each one is rejected from carrying the line of blessing and leadership. The fourth, Judah, will be ancestor to David and to Jesus, and the narratives about him have stunning points of correspondence with each of these most famous descendants.

Finally, I also see the Bible as an icon. Through many trips to Turkey and Greece I have come to appreciate something of the beauty of Eastern Orthodox Christianity. I don't know a great deal about this part of the church, but I do value the ancient use of icons in the soul's approach to God. Literalistic Christians in the Middle Ages destroyed churches that had icons. These are pictures or images of devotional significance and crowds were stirred against them as they were thought to be "graven images," something forbidden in the Old Testament. However, those who value them are clear that they see them not as idols to be worshipped, but as windows into the mystery of God. This, I find, is a good way to see the Bible, too. Don't stop at the literal meaning of the text. Gaze at it slowly. Ask questions. Little by little this approach seems to allow a welcome into an atmosphere of trust. It's not that all questions are given a direct answer; rather, it's a connection of heart and soul with God beyond the issues being faced that gives confidence to go on. A great deal of my academic work revolves around the writings of famous people in church history. It's strange to me how little the early church focused on a heavily literalistic approach to interpretation. This is a modern phenomenon, after the Protestant Reformation. Before that it was possible to say, along with Bernard of Clairvaux, "Only the voice that sings can understand."[4] Perhaps we need to revisit some of the wisdom of the past in order to glean greater wisdom from the Scriptures today.

Chapter Seven
Bringing It Home

It has been, as I indicated at the start, quite a journey. Writing this book has felt that way, too. Both have been journeys of self-discovery and I am grateful for where they have led. I struggled for such a long time to get to a place that seems so obvious and good at this juncture. It is not easy to shake off the shackles of an embedded way of seeing something. But the freedom, once reached, is palpable. In my heart I knew it long before my thinking could find the way. Every time I had a conversation with a gay or lesbian person I knew that I accepted him or her entirely. All I ever wanted to do was to communicate care and respect. But later, on my own, when I thought about the implications of this and what I believed my Scriptures to be saying, I would be so torn.

I believe that it was the writing of Brian McLaren that helped me to see that I had not been treating the Bible in a healthy way. Gradually, this led to a rethink of everything. I had been teaching for decades, based on ideas I found within the text, that the Bible ought not to be a rulebook. I had simply not understood that I was still treating it in this way myself.

I had also known and taught about the power of worldview to influence thought. Gradually I realized that we are all prone to emphasize certain ideas or passages of the Bible and that these, in turn, form a filter system or worldview that controls a good deal of our interpretation. Finally, I decided that the only filter system that is worthy of the character of the Great Subject of the book is mercy and love. Strangely, even in the passage that held me back from total support of gay Christian relationships, Romans 1, the last point on the downward spiral is represented by one word: unmerciful. It comes far past the sexual problems that are depicted in the first two phases of the direction that is being described. Apparently, a hardened heart toward other humans is far worse, in God's eyes, than what we do or do not do, with our own bodies.

Later, as I finally wrestled for myself with the seven references in the Bible that relate to homosexuality, I learned that there is very little likelihood that the Bible had anything to say about loving and committed relationships between people who found, often to their dismay, that they were attracted to their own gender. Two passages in the Old Testament are about gang rape and dominance of outsiders. Two others have to do with a Holiness Code that was for a particular cultural context. There are other facets of our society that would have to be tossed if we believed that all of the things called "abomination" in Leviticus applied to us (including our entire economic system and the eating of lobster). Two passages in the New Testament translate a badly understood term as homosexuality in recent Bibles, even though it is possible to find inferences from history that suggest that the term could relate to a specific act, to idolatry, or to some form of sexual exploitation.

And finally, there is Romans 1. When I studied this passage closely, I realized that it was describing a downward spiral of behaviour that flowed from a darkened understanding of God. Wrong beliefs about God seem to lead to wrong actions from God's perspective. But the point of this passage is that things get worse. It starts with a loosened moral standard that becomes an abnormal moral standard. Finally, it leads to a depraved way of thinking about almost everything. When I considered the flow of the argument, it suddenly seemed obvious to me that the people who have "exchanged the natural function for that which is unnatural" (Romans 1:26) are heterosexuals. These are people who are aiming at greater degrees of sensuality by abandoning their naturally felt or intuitive orientations. As I say, the point of the passage is that things are getting worse. So this is not about the minority of people who, through no choice of their own, are genuinely attracted to their own gender.

That is a nuanced understanding, similar to the issue of slavery. A better perspective will build upon seeds of compassion found in the Bible but will only make sense later in history.

Ironically, the next chapter tells us that no one has the right to judge anyone else because we are all somewhere on this spectrum and all in need of help from God.

It is very likely that the Bible, even if it was a rulebook, has nothing to say about committed and faithful relationships between people of the same gender. But even if it did, the Bible is the place we go to develop a relationship with a loving and merciful God. We are not forced to give two and three thousand year old answers to today's questions. Rather, we look for principles that will help us make mature and beautiful decisions today that we believe are in line with the things God cares about most. For those of us who believe that Jesus Christ is the best demonstration of what this looks like, there can be little doubt that acceptance and inclusion make much more sense than rejection and exclusion.

In my own story, I was helped to see this by Lewis Smedes when he said, "People have to do the best they can with what they have been given," and by Peggy and Tony Campolo's example. They love each other in spite of their disagreement about the best way forward for

LGBT Christians. He says celibacy and she says marriage. But when push comes to shove, and people tell him that they can't live a celibate life, he directs them to her. They both agree that it's better for people to find a partner than it is to live without God, community or morality.

Another voice speaks loudly to me as well. Archbishop Desmond Tutu from South Africa recently wrote this:

> The Jesus I worship is not likely to collaborate with those who vilify and persecute an already oppressed minority. I myself could not have opposed the injustice of penalizing people for something about which they could do nothing—their race—and then have kept quiet as women were being penalized for something they could do nothing about—their gender; hence my support for the ordination of women to the priesthood and the episcopate.
>
> Equally, I cannot keep quiet while people are being penalized for something about which they can do nothing—their sexuality. To discriminate against our sisters and brothers who are lesbian or gay on grounds of their sexual orientation for me is as totally unacceptable and unjust as apartheid ever was.[1]

And all of this has led me to the conviction that marriage ought to be an option for same-gendered couples. Anything less will play into the hands of those who are offended by difference. It is particularly the minority position that must be protected and safeguarded if we want to form a just and compassionate society.

I believe that this is in line with the heart of God as well as with the guiding principles of Scripture. As stories in this book make evident, it can be a very difficult thing for a person to realize that he or she has a different sexual orientation than almost everyone else. People can be overcome by their sense of shame, difference, and rejection. What a wonderful opportunity this provides for the Church of Jesus Christ! He stands in history as the best example of someone who crossed social barriers to welcome and include people who felt like outsiders. It's time for us to follow Him in this. The Bible declares this message very strongly. It's time to learn to interpret toward love.

Endnotes

Chapter 1

1 Caitlin Ryan, David Huebner, Rafael Diaz and Jorge Sanchez, "Family Rejection as a Predictor of Negative Health Outcomes in White and Latino Lesbian, Gay and Bisexual Young Adults," in Pediatrics: Official Journal of the American Academy of Pediatrics, Vol. 123, No. 1, January 1, 2009, 346-352. Available at: <http://pediatrics.aappublications.org/content/123/1/346.long#ref-list-1>, last accessed June 4, 2013.

2 Blaise Pascal, *Pensées*, trans. W. F. Trotter, vol. 33 of Great Books of the Western World, eds. Robert Maynard Hutchins and Mortimer J. Adler (Chicago: Encyclopaedia Britannica, 1952), 222.

3 Thomas C. Oden, *Care of Souls in the Classic Tradition*, ed. Don S. Browning, Theology and Pastoral Care Series (Philadelphia, PA: Fortress Press, 1984), 19.

4 Ibid., 18.

5 Paul G. Hiebert, "Conversion, Culture and Cognitive Categories," *Gospel in Context*, Vol. 1, (October, 1978): 28.

6 George G. Hunter III, *The Celtic Way of Evangelism: How Christianity Can Reach the West ... Again* (Nashville, TN: Abingdon Press, 2000), 53-55.

Chapter 2

1   Brian D. McLaren, *A New Kind of Christianity: Ten Questions that are Transforming the Faith* (New York: HarperOne, 2010), 79.

2   James Gillespie Birney, *The American Churches, The Bulwarks of American Slavery* (Newburyport: Charles Whipple, 1842). Reprinted online at: <http://utc.iath.virginia.edu/christn/chesjgbat.html>, last accessed June 10, 2013.

3   Brian D. McLaren, *A New Kind of Christianity*, 71.

4   Saint Augustine, *Confessions*, trans. R. S. Pine-Coffin (London: Penguin Books, 1961), 303.

5   *Early Christian Writings: The Apostolic Fathers*, trans. Maxwell Staniforth (New York: Dorset Press, 1968), 38-39.

6   S. I. McMillan and David E. Stern, *None of These Diseases: The Bible's Health Secrets for the 21st Century* (Grand Rapids, MI: Fleming H. Revell, 2000), 18-20.

7   Soren Kierkegaard, *Fear and Trembling* (Radford, VA: Wilder Publications, 2008), 39ff.

8   Anthony de Mello, *The Way to Love: Meditations for Life* (New York: Image, Random House, 1992), 34.

9   Martin Buber, *I and Thou*, trans. Walter Kaufmann (New York: Charles Scribner's Sons, 1970), 53ff.

10   St. Gregory the Great, *Pastoral Care*, trans. Henry Davis, Ancient Christian Writers: The Works of the Fathers in Translation, ed. Johannes Quasten and Joseph Plumpe (New York: Newman Press, 1978), 21.

11   Oden, *Care of Souls*, 12.

12   Howard Stone and James Duke, *How to Think Theologically* (Minneapolis, MN: Augsburg Fortress, 1996), 15-16.

13   Ibid., 41.

14   Brian D. McLaren, *A New Kind of Christian: A Tale of Two Friends on a Spiritual Journey* (San Francisco: Jossey-Bass, 2001), 81.

15   Rami Shapiro, *Ethics of the Sages, Pirke Avot: Annotated and Explained* (Woodstock, VT: Skylight Paths Publishing, 2006), 47.

16   Ibid., 47.

17   Lewis Smedes says the same thing in different words in "Exploring the Morality of Homosexuality," chapter 9 in *Homosexuality and Christian Faith*, ed. Walter Wink (Minneapolis, MN: Augsburg Fortress, 1999), 82.

18   Justin Lee, *Torn: Rescuing the Gospel from the Gays-Vs.-Christians Debate* (New York: Jericho Books, 2012), see in particular chapter 6, "Justin in Exgayland", 70ff.

Chapter 3

1   Martin Luther, *The Freedom of a Christian*, trans. W. A. Lambert, revised Harold J. Grimm, in *Three Treatises* (Philadelphia, PA: Fortress Press, 1970), 277.

2   Jack Rogers, *Jesus, the Bible, and Homosexuality: Explode the Myths, Heal the Church, Revised and Expanded Edition* (Louisville, KY: Westminster Knox Press, 2009), 66-68.

3   Sandra Richter, *The Epic of Eden: A Christian Entry into the Old Testament* (Downers Grove, IL: InterVarsity Press, 2008), 24-42.

4   Rogers, *Jesus, the Bible, and Homosexuality*, 68-70.

5   Ibid., 68.

6   Ibid., 70-71.

7   John the Faster, sixth century Patriarch of Constantinople, is widely credited with this usage (see many discussions online). Many scholars have wrestled with the meaning of this word. The safest thing to say about the word is that its meaning is unclear. See Rogers, *Jesus, the Bible, and Homosexuality*, 70-71, and Lee, *Torn*, 183-188.

8   Rogers, *Jesus, the Bible, and Homosexuality*, 72-75; see also Lee, *Torn*, 178-183.

9   Smedes, "Exploring the Morality" in *Homosexuality and Christian Faith*, 78-80, agrees with this position and states it well.

10   Ironically, as Brad Jersak pointed out, this sin of going against natural boundaries is the very thing that churches have asked LGBT people to do. Personal correspondence, June 6, 2013.

11   Matt Croasmun, Elm City Vineyard Church, "Idolatry, Hypocrisy, and the Wrath of God, Romans 1:18-2:16," June 24, 2012, available at: <http://ecvtalks.blogspot.ca/2012_06_01_archive.html>, last accessed June 12, 2013. I am indebted to Dan Bent of Calgary, Alberta, for directing me to this talk.

12   James Fowler, *Becoming Adult, Becoming Christian: Adult Development and Christian Faith* (San Francisco: Jossey-Bass, 2000), 55.

13   N. T. Wright, *The Last Word: Beyond the Bible Wars to a New Understanding of the Authority of Scripture* (New York: HarperCollins, 2005), 123.

14   Ibid., 57.

Chapter 4

1 Lorena Henry, more commonly known as LA, shared a profound insight about this with me: "From my own experience, I have grown immensely as a human being since coming out, but I have struggled with finding a way of grounding my spiritual needs in a spiritual community. Without that community, spiritual growth flounders. Who knows what amazing gay spiritual leaders will develop as/if/when the church embraces LGBTQ people as equal members?" Personal correspondence, June 9, 2013.

2 See Endnote # 1.

3 Jean Vanier, *Community and Growth, Revised Edition* (Mahwah, NJ: Paulist Press, 2003), 51.

4 Dave Schmelzer, Greater Boston Vineyard: "Homosexuality and Churchgoing," February 20, 2011. First talk in Hard Questions Series: <http://vcfaudio.bostonvineyard.org/11022-cambridgesermon.mp3>, last accessed, June 5, 2013.

5 Richard Beck, *Unclean: Meditations on Purity, Hospitality, and Mortality* (Eugene, OR: Cascade Books, 2011), 6.

6 Ibid., 146.

7 Peggy Campolo, "In God's House There are Many Closets," chapter 12 in *Homosexuality and Christian Faith*, ed. Walter Wink (Minneapolis, MN: Augsburg Fortress, 1999), 97-104.

8 Peggy and Tony Campolo, *Sex + Religion*: Episode 12, "Same-sex Attraction," aired Sept. 10, 2012 on eqhd.ca.

9   Lee, *Torn*, 55-62.

10   See Endnote # 22.

11   Smedes, "Exploring the Morality" in *Homosexuality and Christian Faith*, 82.

12   David Anderson, *Gracism: the Art of Inclusion* (Downers Grove, IL: InterVarsity, 2007), 21.

Chapter 5

1   Gregory A. Boyd, *The Myth of a Christian Nation: How the Quest for Political Power is Destroying the Church* (Grand Rapids, MI: Zondervan, 2005), 98-100.

2   Ralph Luker and Penny Russell, *The Papers of Martin Luther King, Jr.*, Vol. III, Birth of a New Age: December 1955—December 1956, ed. Clayborne Carson (London: University of California Press, 1997), 486.

3   Theodore Parker, *Ten Sermons of Religion* (Boston: Crosby, Nichols, and Co., 1853), 84-85.

4   Gwynne Dyer, *Global View*, "World Far More Peaceful than Media Portrays," published in The Saint Croix Courier, Tuesday, May, 28, 2013, Vol. 147, No. 35.

5   Hans Rosling, "200 Countries, 200 Years—The Joy of Stats," BBC Four, available at: <http://www.youtube.com/watch?v=jbkSRLYSojo>, last accessed, June 4, 2013.

6   T. M. Luhrmann, *When God Talks Back: Understanding the American Evangelical Relationship with God* (New York: Alfred A. Knopf, 2012), preface, xv-xvi.

Chapter 6

1 Saint Augustine, *Confessions*, 322.

2 Shawn Achor, "The Happy Secret to Better Work," Video on TED.com, filmed May, 2011, posted February, 2012, TEDx Bloomington, available at: <http://www.ted.com/talks/shawn_achor_the_happy_secret_to_better_work.html>, last accessed June 5, 2013.

3 Desmond Tutu, *No Future Without Forgiveness* (New York: Image, Doubleday, 1999).

4 Jean LeClercq, *Bernard of Clairvaux: Selected Works*, trans. G. R. Evans, introduction by Jean LeClercq, preface by Ewert H. Cousins, The Classics of Western Spirituality Series (New York: Paulist Press, 1987), 34.

Chapter 7

1 Desmond Tutu, *God is Not a Christian: And Other Provocations*, excerpt from Chapter Six, "All, All are God's Children: On Including Gays and Lesbians in the Church and Society" (New York: HarperCollins, 2011).

Selected Bibliography

Achor, Shawn. "The Happy Secret to Better Work." Video on TED.com. Filmed May, 2011. Posted February, 2012. TEDx Bloomington. Available at: <http://www.ted.com/talks/shawn_achor_the_happy_secret_to_better_work.html>.

Anderson, David. *Gracism: the Art of Inclusion*. Downers Grove, IL: InterVarsity, 2007.

Augustine, Saint. *Confessions*. Translated by R. S. Pine-Coffin. London: Penguin Books, 1961.

Beck, Richard. *Unclean: Meditations on Purity, Hospitality, and Mortality*. Eugene, OR: Cascade Books, 2011.

Bernard, Saint. *Bernard of Clairvaux: Selected Works*. Translated and with a foreword by G. R. Evans. Introduction by Jean LeClercq. Preface by Ewert H. Cousins. The Classics of Western Spirituality Series. New York: Paulist Press, 1987.

Birney, James Gillespie. *The American Churches, The Bulwarks of American Slavery*. Newburyport: Charles Whipple, 1842. Reprinted online at <http://utc.iath.virginia.edu/christn/chesjgbat.html>, last accessed June 10, 2013.

Boyd, Gregory, A. *The Myth of a Christian Nation: How the Quest for Political Power is Destroying the Church*. Grand Rapids, MI: Zondervan, 2005.

Buber, Martin. *I and Thou*. Translated and with an introduction by Walter Kaufmann. New York: Charles Scribner's Sons, 1970.

Campolo, Peggy. "In God's House There are Many Closets." Chapter 12 in *Homosexuality and Christian Faith*. Edited by Walter Wink. Minneapolis, MN: Augsburg Fortress, 1999.

Clement of Rome. "The First Epistle of Clement to the Corinthians." Chapter in *Early Christian Writings: The Apostolic Fathers*. Translated by Maxwell Staniforth. New York: Dorset Press, 1968.

Croasmun, Matt. "Idolatry, Hypocrisy, and the Wrath of God, Romans 1:18-2:16." Elm City Vineyard Church: June 24, 2012. Available at: <http://ecvtalks.blogspot.ca/2012_06_01_archive.html>.

De Mello, Anthony. *The Way to Love: Meditations for Life*. New York: Image, Random House, 1992.

Dyer, Gwynne. *Global View*, "World Far More Peaceful than Media Portrays." Published in The Saint Croix Courier: Tuesday, May, 28, 2013. Vol. 147, No. 35.

Fowler, James. *Becoming Adult, Becoming Christian: Adult Development and Christian Faith*. San Francisco: Jossey-Bass, 2000.

Gregory the Great, Saint. *Pastoral Care*. Translated and with an introduction by Henry Davis. Ancient Christian Writers: The Works of the Fathers in Translation. Edited by Johannes Quasten and Joseph Plumpe. New York: Newman Press, 1978.

Hiebert, Paul, G. "Conversion, Culture and Cognitive Categories." *Gospel in Context*: Vol. 1, (October, 1978).

Hunter, George, G. III. *The Celtic Way of Evangelism: How Christianity Can Reach the West ... Again*. Nashville, TN: Abingdon Press, 2000.

Kierkegaard, Soren. *Fear and Trembling: A Philosophical Masterpiece*. Radford, VA: Wilder Publications, 2008.

Lee, Justin. *Torn: Rescuing the Gospel from the Gays-Vs.-Christians Debate*. New York: Jericho Books, 2012.

Luhrmann, T. M. *When God Talks Back: Understanding the American Evangelical Relationship with God*. New York: Alfred A. Knopf, 2012.

Luker, Ralph and Penny Russell. *The Papers of Martin Luther King, Jr.* Vol. III, Birth of a New Age: December 1955—December 1956. Edited by Clayborne Carson. London: University of California Press, 1997.

Luther, Martin. "The Freedom of a Christian." Translated by W. A. Lambert. Revised by Harold J. Grimm. Chapter in *Three Treatises*. Philadelphia, PA: Fortress Press, 1970.

McLaren, Brian. *A New Kind of Christian: A Tale of Two Friends on a Spiritual Journey*. San Francisco: Jossey-Bass, 2001.

_____. *A New Kind of Christianity: Ten Questions that are Transforming the Faith*. New York: HarperOne, 2010.

McMillan, S. I. and David E. Stern. *None of These Diseases: The Bible's Health Secrets for the 21st Century*. Grand Rapids, MI: Fleming H. Revell, 2000.

Oden, Thomas C. *Care of Souls in the Classic Tradition*. Edited by Don S. Browning. Theology and Pastoral Care Series. Philadelphia, PA: Fortress Press, 1984.

Parker, Theodore. *Ten Sermons of Religion*. Boston: Crosby, Nichols, and Co., 1853.

Pascal, Blaise. *Pensées*. Translated by W. F. Trotter. Vol. 33, Great Books of the Western World. Edited by Robert Maynard Hutchins and Mortimer J. Adler. Chicago: Encyclopaedia Britannica, 1952.

Richter, Sandra. *The Epic of Eden: A Christian Entry into the Old Testament*. Downers Grove, IL: InterVarsity Press, 2008.

Rogers, Jack. *Jesus, the Bible, and Homosexuality: Explode the Myths, Heal the Church*. Revised and Expanded Edition. Louisville, KY: Westminster Knox Press, 2009.

Rosling, Hans. "200 Countries, 200 Years—The Joy of Stats." BBC Four. Available at: <http://www.youtube.com/watch?v=jbkSRLYSojo>.

Ryan, Caitlin with David Huebner, Rafael Diaz, and Jorge Sanchez. "Family Rejection as a Predictor of Negative Health Outcomes in White and Latino Lesbian, Gay, and Bisexual Young Adults." In Pediatrics: Official Journal of the American Academy of Pediatrics: Vol. 123, No. 1, January 1, 2009, pp. 346-352. Available at <http://pediatrics.aappublications.org/content/123/1/346.long#ref-list-1>.

Selected Bibliography

Schmelzer, David. "Homosexuality and Churchgoing." Greater Boston Vineyard: February 20, 2011. First talk in Hard Questions Series. Available at: <http://vcfaudio.bostonvineyard.org/11022-cambridgesermon.mp3>.

Sex + Religion: Episode 12. "Same-sex Attraction." Television interview with Peggy and Tony Campolo. Aired Sept. 10, 2013 on eqhd.ca.

Shapiro, Rami. *Ethics of the Sages, Pirke Avot: Annotated and Explained*. Woodstock, VT: Skylight Paths Publishing, 2006.

Smedes, Lewis. "Exploring the Morality of Homosexuality." Chapter 9 in *Homosexuality and Christian Faith*. Edited by Walter Wink. Minneapolis, MN: Augsburg Fortress, 1999.

Stone, Howard and James Duke. *How to Think Theologically*. Minneapolis, MN: Augsburg Fortress, 1996.

Tutu, Desmond. *God is Not a Christian: And Other Provocations*. Chapter Six, "All, All are God's Children: On Including Gays and Lesbians in the Church and Society." New York: HarperCollins, 2011.

_____. *No Future Without Forgiveness*. New York: Image, Doubleday, 1999.

Vanier, Jean. *Community and Growth*. Revised Edition. Mahwah, NJ: Paulist Press, 2003.

Wright, N. T. *The Last Word: Beyond the Bible Wars to a New Understanding of the Authority of Scripture*. New York: HarperCollins, 2005.

Made in the USA
Middletown, DE
09 February 2017